770.924 C758t   FV
CONSTANTINE
TINA MODOTTI : A FRAGILE LIFE
                      35.00

St. Louis Community College

Library

5801 Wilson Avenue
St. Louis, Missouri 63110

TINA MODOTTI

**PADDINGTON
PRESS LTD**

THE TWO CONTINENTS
PUBLISHING GROUP

TINA
A Fragile Life

An illustrated biography
by Mildred Constantine

MODOTTI

ENDPAPERS: Fiesta in Huichitlan, Oaxaca, Bullfight Arena, by Tina Modotti, c.1926

Library of Congress Cataloging in Publication Data
Constantine, Mildred.
  Tina Modotti: a fragile life.
  Bibliography: p. 219
  1. Modotti, Tina, 1896–1942.
TR140.M58C66   770′.92′4 [B]   73–20956
ISBN 0–8467–0027–1

ISBN 0–8467–0027–1
Library of Congress Catalog Card Number 73–20956
Copyright 1975 Paddington Press Ltd
Phototypeset by Tradespools Ltd, Frome, Somerset
Printed in the U.S.A.

Designed by Richard Browner

IN THE UNITED STATES
PADDINGTON PRESS LTD
TWO CONTINENTS PUBLISHING GROUP
30 East 42 Street
New York City, N.Y. 10017

IN THE UNITED KINGDOM
PADDINGTON PRESS LTD
1 Wardour Street
London W1

IN CANADA
distributed by
RANDOM HOUSE OF CANADA LTD
370 Alliance Avenue
Toronto, Ontario

CONTENTS

For my Daughters
Judith and Vicki

ACKNOWLEDGMENTS

I wish to acknowledge with deep gratitude the knowledge, generosity, and encouragement, of the people who have helped to turn a legend into a portrait of a woman.

This book is based partly on interviews with people who knew Tina Modotti and whose memories served me well: Manuel Alvarez Bravo, Anita Brenner, Isabel Carbajal, Jean Charlot, Emily Edwards, Jay Leyda, Rosendo Gómez Lorenzo, Yolanda Magrini, Federico Marín, Pablo O'Higgins, Carlos Orozco Romero, María Marín de Orozco, Gustavo Ortiz Hernán, Victor Velarde and Vittorio Vidali. Vidali and Yolanda Magrini have also contributed documents, memorabilia, and photographs, The Weston archive in Carmel, California has the original letters from Tina to Edward Weston from which I have quoted; Cole and Neil Weston have been helpful and cooperative. Ben Maddow has been a profound inspiration in the writing of this work. Alastair Reid has written the beautiful translation of a section of Pablo Neruda's poem. Arthur A. Cohen and Eve Arnold have read the manuscript and provided more detached criticism than I could ever have made.

Ralph W. Bettelheim, my husband, whose spirit and wisdom accompanied me from the moment we both discovered the first firm thread of Tina's life, deserves most of my thanks for his patience and devotion to this work.

M. C.

INTRODUCTION

She was not a leader but she lived with direction and goal; she was not a woman who changed history but she always was at the center of a drama. She seems, whether in pleasure or in anguish, to have had a secret instinct for the limelight.

If there is a public image of Tina Modotti, it is based on gossipy notations of a few chroniclers offering mere notoriety. To certain brief acquaintances, Tina Modotti is known only as the apprentice, model and mistress of the great American photographer Edward Weston. A great and flamboyant beauty, a woman of many loves and numerous escapades, she was proclaimed a great mystery.

I met Tina Modotti for the first and only time in 1941. A close American friend, a Quaker living in Mexico, invited me to a meeting of the *Alianza Antifascista Guiseppe Garibaldi* and casually mentioned that we would have coffee with Tina

Modotti after the meeting. I do not know what image of her I had conjured up in my own mind. When we shook hands and she welcomed me in English I was overwhelmed.

I had prepared myself for this meeting. I knew something of her story: that she had been expelled from Mexico; that she had lived in the Soviet Union; that she had been in Spain all during the Civil War; and that she had returned to Mexico with her companion Carlos Contreras, whom I had met on a separate occasion. She was a small, fragile, silent woman. I hardly dared to ask the many questions I had about her photography. I did not feel that her silence was born either of serenity or timidity, but that she seemed tragically tired. I could see the beauty I had been prepared for in spite of what seemed to be an anguished look in her eyes. The meeting did little more for me than to give Tina Modotti a face and compound the mystery of her.

Not long after this meeting, my American friend wrote to tell me that Tina had died. She cautioned me not to believe rumors I might hear, and sent me a brochure printed in Mexico after Tina's death. This brochure yielded some facts hitherto unknown to me and enlarged on other information.

> Tina was an Italian who had come to the United States in 1913.
> Tina had been married to an American.
> Tina had been an actress in Hollywood.
> Tina had been Weston's apprentice, model and companion and they had lived in Mexico from 1923 to 1926.
> Tina had been the companion of a Cuban, Julio Antonio Mella, who had been assassinated in Mexico.
> Tina was expelled from Mexico in 1930.

Tina had been in the Soviet Union.
Tina had been in Spain—known as Maria—during
the Spanish Civil War from 1935–1939.
Tina had returned to Mexico in 1939 and died there in
1942.

Her name and some of her photographs had been known to
me even before my first visit to Mexico in 1936. The Mexican
artists who were at work in New York on the Federal Arts
Project mural had told me of their program of murals for
public buildings which had begun in the early 1920's. Through
the magazine *Mexican Folkways*, I had seen photographs by
Tina Modotti of some of these painted walls. These composi-
tions were impressive, as were her photographs of Mexican
children, colonial sculpture and folk art.

My primary reason for going to Mexico was the pursuit of
my graduate studies in Mexican colonial art. In retrospect I
realize that this was also to be my first adventure out of my own
country and that I too was on a search. The modern Mexico I
encountered revealed a cultural and social current that aston-
ished me. I was little prepared for the unity of spirit I found
there. It was inevitable, given the times and social conditions in the United States, that I should respond to the aesthetic
and political convictions expressed by the people I encountered
and by the modern Mexican art movement. With great
alacrity I abandoned the old and tried to absorb the new; it
was not the colonial past but the dramatic present that stirred
my imagination and interest.

Arriving at the height of the second surge of mural art in
Mexico, I eagerly sought out the artists engaged in this work.
David Alfaro Siqueiros was in Spain—the Civil War had begun

and he was among the first to volunteer. Diego Rivera was too inaccessible to an art history student, in spite of the fact that while on the staff of the College Art Association I had helped to organize a defense of the Detroit murals. Not daring to use the camera myself, I tried to find Tina Modotti or someone who knew her work. I made inquiries of friends: Frances Toor, the editor of *Mexican Folkways*, Pablo O'Higgins and Leopoldo Mendez, both artists who were engaged in the mural movement and also working with the *Talleres de Gráfica Popular*, and Gustavo Ortiz Hernán, who was then on the staff of the newspaper *El Universal*. All I could learn was that Modotti was no longer in Mexico. There was mention of her being somewhere in Europe. There were also stories of her having been a Hollywood actress who had lived in Mexico with Edward Weston (a name only vaguely known to me at that time), and of her numerous lovers, although they were never named. Almost everyone mentioned her beauty, although no one seemed to have a photograph of her. In the Rivera murals in Chapingo I could see the panels "Virgin Soil" and "Germination" for which she had been the model. The stories were not like the tales of rumormongers, which always seem to be replete with more information—fact or fiction. The legend of Tina Modotti began at that time.

As I pursued my research into Mexican art of the twenties I kept encountering Tina's work—photographs in the book on Rivera's frescoes, Carleton Beal's article in *Creative Arts*. I had no idea of her age, or of her nationality, or of her face. She had simply become part of the mythology of the modern Mexico that I was trying to investigate.

The years since my first visit had been filled with more work and travel in Mexico, with participating in the excitement of the New Deal; my growing political consciousness brought me to work for the Loyalists in the Spanish Civil War and other anti-Fascist causes. Then in 1946 the first major exhibition of Edward Weston's photographs was held at the Museum of Modern Art in New York. Included were some splendid romantic photographs of Tina's hands and her beautiful strong face. By 1949 I was at work at the Museum of Modern Art, and fortunate enough to be again under the guidance of Rene d'Harnoncourt, then the Director. I had known him since the early thirties, when he brought a fine exhibition of Mexican art to the United States, and had learned much from him about Mexican culture of the past as well as the present. He had lived and worked in Mexico during the exciting twenties, and had met Weston and Modotti in 1925. He was convinced of the greatness of Weston's work and of Tina's sure, growing talent. He too had heard of her death and of those vague rumors. The Museum had begun to acquire prints of Weston's work, and in the late fifties several by Tina had come into the collection. When the first volume of Weston's Daybooks was published in 1961, I avidly read his almost day-by-day account of those years in Mexico. Somehow the veil had been lifted only enough to make me more curious about this woman. There was enough information about her to make me know that there had been a major shift in values from those she had when she came to Mexico in 1923.

In 1971 I embarked on a search for Tina Modotti's photographs for a projected exhibition of her work at the Museum of Modern Art. This led me to a search for the story of her life. Not too surprisingly, Mexico in 1971 was far different from the disputatious and divided Mexico of 1941. Thirty years had softened attitudes, and people were more willing—even eager —to reminisce about the past. It is impossible to account for or to intuit the whole of Tina's life. Yet I found, as I retraced my own past in the world of Mexico's artists and intellectuals, that I could jog many memories of that safely distant period.

My searches were based on a few questions: what are the facts, what are the mysteries in the life of Tina Modotti? How was she different from other women of her time? What control did she have over her own destiny and those close to her? What motivated the human and political feelings that find such rich expression in her work? And what about the multitudinous rumors about her death: that she had been killed in a car in Mexico; that she had been poisoned; that she had left the Soviet Union for Rumania and was murdered there; that she had been purged in Moscow in the thirties.

The world of art is indeed a very small one, and I found that my life since the early thirties had been touched by many of the same people who knew Tina Modotti.

Each person I interviewed led me to another. I dispatched a letter to Vittorio Vidali (whom I had known in Mexico as Carlos Contreras) in Trieste, where he has been living since the late forties. He generously gave me documents, newspaper clippings and photographs hitherto unknown to me. He also shared his knowledge and memories of his dead companion. He sent me on to Udine where Tina was born. There the *Circolo Culturale* had reprinted the brochure originally published in Mexico with additional photographs. I went back to the United States to meet Yolanda Magrini, Tina's youngest sister, who is living in California. Yolanda is the last of the

Modotti family, and she gave me complete access to family photographs as well as her memories of her childhood.

Returning to Mexico, and now armed with more information, I again met with Manuel Alvarez Bravo, Anita Brenner, Federico Marín, María and Carlos Orozco Romero, Fernando Gamboa, Angélica Arenal de Siqueiros, Gustavo Ortiz Hernán, and Gómez Lorenzo.

The archives of the newspaper *Excelsior* were made available to me so that I could follow the day-by-day reporting on the assassination of Mella. Ben Maddow in Los Angeles was at work on his brilliant biography of Edward Weston. He not only helped to clarify salient points, but also made available to me copies of many letters Tina had written to Weston.

Each day brought a new clue; an unexpected chain of information grew. People seemed happy to know that Tina Modotti might be "resurrected" and recognized for herself and her work. In spite of the fact that many imponderables remained, I began to put the jigsaw of her life together.

Tina Modotti was a vital spirit in one of the most creative and evocative periods of the twentieth century. She was a woman created by many forces. She was a force in the life of a great photographer as well as a highly talented photographer in her own right. Yet her work is known and recognized by only a small number of appreciative colleagues and historians. Seen up to now only through a shimmering veil, the woman Tina Modotti deserves to be brought sharply into focus, to be revealed as the gifted artist and the ardent revolutionary. I now feel that the veil has been lifted on that "fragile" life of iron!

Mildred Constantine

Tina, San Francisco. c.1918

1896-1923
Italy: Udine
USA: San Francisco, Los Angeles

Passport No. 23.922 was issued in Barcelona, Spain, on December 21, 1937. It described the holder—Dra. Carmen Ruiz Sánchez—as a widow, professor by profession, with brown eyes, brown hair and oval face. This passport, valid for France, was renewed in Barcelona on January 21, 1939, marked for "*todo el mundo*" except Germany, Italy, Portugal, Austria and Hungary. The woman was fleeing from Spain. She traveled from Figueras on February 3, 1939, to France with a visa from the Agence Consular de France. There she received a visa dated March 15, 1939 from the Mexican Legation in Paris. An American transit visa was given to her by the American consulate in Paris on March 27, allowing her to disembark on arrival in New York. Sailing from Cherbourg on the "Queen Mary" on April 1, she was denied permission, despite the transit visa, to disembark in New York. Finally, on April 19,

1939, she arrived at Vera Cruz, Mexico.

Tina Modotti was returning to Mexico with absolutely authentic false papers, a little less than ten years after being expelled. She was returning to the country that had been "home" for almost a decade of her brief, intense and creative life.

This hegira from war-torn Spain to asylum in the revolutionary Mexico of President Lázaro Cárdenas was one of many she had been forced to make in her life. How many times in a lifetime can you begin to live?

Tina Modotti was many things: a gifted photographer, passionate companion of artists and revolutionaries, fighter for the cause of humanity, "Maria" who succored the children and wounded in Spain, the tempestuous beauty of unabashed sensuality. Who was she? Dead, she is a legend poeticized and victimized by conjecture, anecdotes and, where fact is lacking, imaginative embellishments.

It is difficult—almost impossible—to reconcile the woman Tina Modotti with the picture conjured up by those who knew her slightly, who freely gossiped and drew verbal pictures that are part of the literature and legends about her. That she was beautiful all agree.

Yet nothing so aggravated Tina as the references to her beauty. That she was aware of it one can be sure; it probably was her immediate passport into the Hollywood scene of 1920. On the other hand, she always had a sense of personal identity, and the Hollywood image of her as "femme fatale" suited neither her innate sense of dignity nor her earnest desire to be an actress.

That she was able to arouse admiration, passion and desire in men is not surprising. That she was able to arouse admiration for her beauty in the women whom she met is both a tribute to her and to them. Apparently, it did not obscure their perception of her talent as an artist or her strength and honesty as a woman.

As Tina's revolutionary awareness grew and she came increasingly to identify herself with political action, so, it seems, grew her resentment against those who spoke of her beauty.— She was to state at the time of her deportation, "I could not possibly see what 'prettiness' had to do with the revolutionary movement . . . evidently women here [New Orleans] are measured by a motion picture star standard." Obviously her earlier Hollywood experience still rankled.

In the many photographs Edward Weston made of Tina, the tempestuous beauty which Kenneth Rexroth claimed for her hardly appears.

> There was a cafe where they all hung out with heavily armed politicians, bullfighters, criminals, prostitutes and burlesque girls. The most spectacular person of all was a photographer, artist's model, high class courtesan, and Mata Hari for the Comintern, Tina Modotti. She was the heroine of a lurid political assassination and was what I guess is called an international beauty. I had outgrown my fondness for the Kollantai type and she terrified me. She was exterminated in the Great Purge[1].

Aleksandra Mikhailovna Kollantai was a Russian revolutionist. She traveled internationally on propaganda missions which kept her away from her own country until the 1917 revolution, when she returned to assume a diplomatic post. She was a USSR minister to Mexico until 1928 (did she and Tina ever meet?). She was a proponent, in her novels and in her life, of a single standard of morality for men and women.

Rexroth was writing of a time in the late 1920's when he was in Mexico. In one paragraph he invented facts to suit his own fancy or need for fictionalizing events which happened long after his brief observations of this woman. Unhappily, later writers have often injudiciously quoted the Kollantai reference. And facts give the lie to his wishful inventions. Yet one person's malice often suffices to reinforce misconceptions and create a myth.

There is no fully detailed tapestry of the life of Tina Modotti. It cannot be unraveled, examined, evaluated. Facts, like bits of string, must first be entwined, and the lengths of twine must be overlapped and thickened to provide the rich warp and weft of her life. What are the implications of her strong yet vulnerable gaze, of her unrepressed sexuality, of the perseverence and fatalism which did not permit her to be reconciled to her own fate or to that of humanity?

She was a woman, she was an Italian. She did not set out to be a radical nonconformist. There was a personal, aesthetic and political order to the life of Tina Modotti. Each part had a specific shape. Each part was wedded to the other by her commitments. She chose to identify herself with the arts, with the poor and with the solidarity of the revolution. Instinct and upbringing, with its rites and rituals, and the fact of her birthplace had prepared her for all that. Undeniable intelligence and fortitude directed her ambitions and helped to create the vital points of relationship between Tina and society.

Assunta Adelaide Luigia Modotti—always called Tina—was born in Udine, Italy, on August 16, 1896. Udine, the capital of the province of Friuli, is situated at the foot of the Alps. Its location northeast of Venice makes it a strategic point between the approach to the Adriatic on the south and to Austria on the north. It has a profoundly Latin population and at the time of Tina's birth had a predominantly feudal society with a long history of social unrest. It is a medieval city of classical palaces, piazzas, fountains, ancient markers with roads and streets that run up to the hills. Udine's climate, and the vegetation in the mountains and hills encourage extensive land cultivation. The Friuliani are hard-working, hard-playing people. They are passionate, yet not as garrulous as most other Italians. One feels they are a people of an ancient and civilized heritage.

In this small, peaceful town, the people knew intimately the section in which they lived. Democracy was at work in the schools, at play in the streets and in the taverns. The houses, mainly sixteenth- and seventeenth-century buildings, were lived in by a cross-section of the population. Those of wealth and social standing lived in the "piano nobile" (palatial floor) of these old houses, while the tradesmen and artisans lived, together with their families, in their shops on the ground floor level. One was always aware of the countryside. Vegetable and flower gardens flourished; roads led gently toward the hills or to the center of town. There was communion in the streets: the children of all families attended the same schools (if indeed they went to school) and played together in the streets. On Sundays the workers' families and children were all dressed in their finery and indistinguishable from the more bourgeois townsfolk. The women met to do their laundry in the public canals, and the men gathered in the taverns.

The ordinary working man searched his way through many

paths, eagerly embracing the essential contradictions in his life. He was generally poor but progressive, and maintained an inner dignity. Those who did not till the soil worked as carpenters, blacksmiths and bricklayers. When such work was scarce, they would go out for seasonal work. They went out because of need, because of tradition, but they also went with pride and with hope for their future.

By instinct of class, a Friuliano was a socially conscious being—a revolutionary through the Socialist party. He would have had contact with labor struggles through his proximity to Austria and to the industrialization going on in the province of Lombardy. Tina's youngest sister, Yolanda, relates Tina's nostalgic memories of her childhood, when her father carried her on his shoulders as he participated in the noisy May Day demonstrations.

Giuseppe Modotti and his wife Assunta lived with their six children: the girls, Mercedes, Tina, Yolanda, Giaconda; the boys, Benvenuto and Giuseppe. Of this family only Yolanda Magrini remains. Yolanda is a tiny, spirited, beautiful seventy-two-year-old woman who lives in a plant- and flower-filled home in Southern California. She is still the politically aware and active representative of her family tradition.

Seeking work in Austria, Giuseppe moved his family there for several years. They remained there until Tina was nine years old. Returning to Udine, Tina's father continued to work as a mason. When he had saved enough money he left his Family behind and emigrated to the United States, settling in San Francisco. Tina, the second eldest child, worked in a textile factory to help support her mother and the younger children.

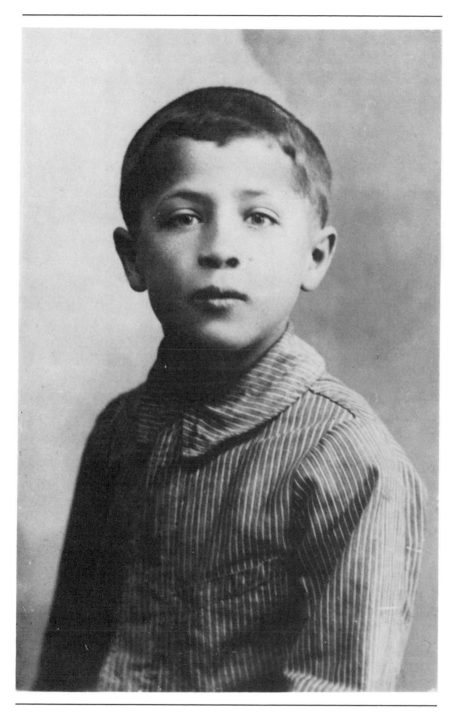

Benvenuto Modotti, Tina's brother. Photo by P. Modotti, Udine. c.1915
(Perhaps a relative who interested Tina in the camera)

According to Paul Radin, writing in 1935, the Italian coming to California experienced less discrimination in the nineteenth century than other minority groups which had arrived during the mining days. Andrew Rollo, writing in 1968, also described life for the Italians who went West as neither disappointing nor miserable. "In general, there were no slums, crowding and little prejudice." According to Rollo, the Italian colony was self-sufficient to a large degree "partly because it wanted to be and partly because it was constrained to be."

Rollo says that Italian immigrants maintained strong family ties and habitually married within their own groups. There was little change of occupation or uprooting of the values inculcated in Italy. Bakeries, groceries, banks, cafes, restaurants, lawyers, were all in the self-contained world of little Italy. Of the almost 17,000 Italians in San Francisco, over half were Northern Italians. They had their own newspapers and, by the 1900's, their own theatrical groups, opera companies. While they were considered active participants in the life of the city, they constituted a world unto themselves.

On the other hand, it is acknowledged that well before the United States entered World War I, workers' conditions in California were extremely bad. Over-long working hours and bad housing facilities created strikes which brought violence from both sides.

Giuseppe Modotti, having had contact with the labor struggles in Italy, was certainly responsive to the conditions of workers who, like himself, had been neglected by the craft unions and were laboring under unfair conditions. The Italians in California found that almost everything grown in the old country could be grown in San Francisco, and the importance of San Francisco as a Pacific port was greatly increased by the Spanish-American War. Still, artisans such as carpenters and masons were no more secure as wage-earners than they had been in Italy.

Nevertheless, the eldest daughter was able to join her father, and by 1913 Giuseppe Modotti had earned enough money to send for Tina, who left for California in a third-class boat full of Italian immigrants. She was just seventeen years old. Removal to a new world did not alter the need to work—or her will to do so. About a week after arrival in San Francisco, she began to work in a textile factory. What life was like after the entire family had finally emigrated to San Francisco several years later is best described by her youngest sister, Yolanda. She recalls, in speaking of Tina,

> When she was only a young girl, she looked to me, younger as I was, like a little lady, with those big, sad eyes in a hunger-stricken face. She was the only one among the six of us who worked and made a few pennies a day. She used to work twelve hours a day in a silk factory, and whatever her duties were, her fingers were always swollen and sore. One night, in early winter, our fire and candles had gone out, as it would often happen. My mother and I were waiting for Tina, clinging to each other in order to keep warm. We were sad and dejected because there was nothing to eat. When we would have food, I would run to meet Tina, anxious to tell her the good news.
>
> Our main concern throughout our childhood was to have something to eat, for we did not have any toys and we could never find the time to enjoy ourselves.

Our youngest brother would often cry when, back from school, he would realize that there was nothing to eat; but Tina never said anything, quietly going to bed right after coming home from work . . .

Even as a young child in Italy, and later in the United States, Tina was endowed with a deep sense of responsibility toward her family. Leaving the factory to seek more remunerative work, she turned to dressmaking and made deliveries for additional income.

In spite of the poverty, long hours of work, the insufficiency of food, this period of life in the United States opened many new directions for Tina. The woman's suffrage movement from 1910 onward gave women new freedom to function outside the household. This new atmosphere obviously encouraged Tina's independence, and she began to take part in amateur theatrical activity in the Italian quarter. Her father was an amateur musician and he also participated in the theater and stree fiestas. Rene Dubos has written that San Francisco

> . . . developed without Puritan influence. However, it was soon given a special character by the large number of immigrants who came to it from Northern Italy. Unlike poor Sicilians and Neapolitans, these North Italians had a great awareness of European culture and created an atmosphere similar to that of cosmopolitan Mediterranean harbors but without the Mediterranean poverty . . . .
>
> Not having arisen as a WASP settlement, San Francisco acquired from the beginning the mood of a large European continental city, with sections where anybody could engage in behavior of his own choice,

no matter how far out. Indifference toward conventional mores and openness to cultural innovation made it a mecca for persons in search of new life styles . . . .[2]

Perhaps it was the general as well as a personal search for a new direction in her life that prompted Tina to fall in love with an American poet and painter of French Canadian background. Roubaix de L'Abrie Richéy was tall, slender, with a dark moustache and large eyes. We know little about him except that he came from a large family which had been in America for over a generation and had resided first in New Orleans, and then in Los Angeles. They met, Yolanda recalls, at a function at the Pan Pacific International Exposition in San Francisco in 1915.

Approximately two years later they were married and moved to Los Angeles, setting up their home in Richéy's studio. Tina, ever the conscientious wage-earner, continued her dressmaking. Richéy pursued his painting and his poetry, but with an uncertainty about both activities.

Was this marriage a way out of Tina's particular ghetto, and did she hope through it to assimilate herself into American life? What insight we have into Richéy is gained from the lovely photograph which Weston made. This picture captures perfectly the romantic aura which surrounded him. The flowing tie, the shy, downward, indirect gaze, the hands and only part of the face illuminated, confirm Tina's own description of him:

a young boy with eyes dimmed by dreams . . . overwhelmed by that vague "something" which is present at all times for the soul sensitive enough to perceive it. And it was no doubt the overpowering force of his sen-

Tina and Robo at home, Los Angeles. 1921

Tina and Robo with his family, Los Angeles. 1921

sitive emotions and sensibilities that made him turn to art and pursue it as an outlet and a means of expression. As he grew up, all his artistic fervor pervaded his whole being and personality. All of himself was his personality . . . . he always attracted attention for his simple charm and gentle manners. Never part of a crowd nor happy amid one, he was at his best in the company of a few intimate and sympathetic friends.[3]

Tina herself was not content to remain a dressmaker. Whether it was through her earlier experience as an amateur actress that she was "discovered" by the Hollywood film world is not entirely certain. We know that she was ambitious and interested in dramatics, and it must have been logical, given her beauty, to seek a future in Hollywood. Certainly her search for self-expression might have found an outlet in acting, and it was a profession more lucrative than dressmaking. Her beauty, acknowledged by all who knew her, must have given her access to Hollywood. In later years, as she became Weston's model, she must have been aware of the electrifying effect her beauty had on those around her. Did she consciously make use of this power? We have already seen how even women commented on and enjoyed her beauty and how, as her political awareness grew, her abhorrence of references to her beauty was readily expressed.

However Tina entered the world of Hollywood, in 1920 she was featured in several films. She was always costumed as a a gypsy or harem girl, in the typical Hollywood version of the female "heavy" of the era. But this typecasting did not appeal to Tina. "The exotic allure of Tina Modotti," proclaimed in a poster for *The Tiger's Eye*, (1920) exploited nothing more than

This picture and the seven that follow are of Tina in Hollywood, 1920–21

her physical attributes. This crude exploitation was limiting and offensive to both her dignity and her aspirations. As Weston put it when they happened upon one of her films in Mexico, "We had a good laugh over the villainous character she portrayed. The brains and imaginations of our movie directors cannot picture an Italian girl except with a knife in her teeth and blood in her eye."[4]

The post-war period in Los Angeles saw a clash between the smugness of the people who carried on the old traditions and those who sought the new. The different strata of people ranged from those who had carried their Midwestern habits with them, to the new immigrants, to those who were pioneering and hoped to find fertile ground for their ideas.

Robo's studio (her husband was called Robo by all who knew him) was something of a gathering place for Bohemian writers and artists with radical points of view. All had in common the need to attack the status quo of the time. They sought personal and sexual independence as a requisite to artistic expression, and carried on endless discussions about contemporary music, dance, literature and art. Together they explored psychoanalysis, socialism, and the religious movements—from Hinduism to Christian Science—which had begun to take root in Los Angeles. They banded together to make each feel that he was not alone and not simply floating through life. They cooly indulged in appraising each other, in self-expression and drinking in the complexities of the times—of Joyce, Pound, Freud—with a restless vitality.

Among those who met in the Richéys' studio in 1921 were Ramiel McGehee, a writer; Sadakichi Hartmann (Sidney Allen), a film and photography critic; Edward Weston, photographer; Margrethe Mather, photographer; and the Mexican archaeologist Ricardo Gómez Robelo, who was at that time head of the Fine Arts Department of Mexico. Other Mexican artists and intellectuals were frequent guests as well, and they brought stimulating reports of the reemergence of the Mexican Indian past and the exciting possibilities offered by the revolution of their day—a revolution expressed in cultural as well as social terms. In reponse to an invitation from Gómez Robelo, Robo left in December 1921 for Mexico, where he hoped to find an environment better suited to his temperament. As Tina was to write so movingly after Robo's death: "With an intentional disregard for the modern spirit of this age and of this country in particular (the United States), attracted by the beauty and the charm of the past still lingering there . . . he found sympathy and romance . . . but only for a little while."[5]

Whether it was through McGehee's contacts with the movie colony, as suggested by Ben Maddow, that Weston first met Tina, a "truly extraordinary woman who was to shatter and then reconstruct his life" (Introduction, Daybook No. 1), or whether their first meeting took place in Robo's studio is not certain.

We do know from a letter which Tina wrote to Weston on April 25 of that same year that their affair had begun before Robo had left for Mexico. In the letter Tina had written, "One night after—all day I have been intoxicated with the memory of last night and overwhelmed with the beauty and madness of it . . . How can I wait until we meet again!" That this affair was adulterous for both Tina and Weston did not lessen the beauty; indeed it contributed to the madness. In a response to one of

Weston's letters, Tina said:

> Once more I have been reading your letter and as at every other time my eyes are full of tears—I never realized before that a letter—a mere sheet of paper— could be such a spiritual thing—could emanate so much feeling—you gave a soul to it! Oh! If I could be with you now at this hour I love so much, I would try to tell you how much beauty has been added to my life lately! When may I come over? I am waiting for your call.

This is undoubtedly the first in the long series of letters which Tina and Weston exchanged. This communication is remarkable both for the unselfconscious passion, the exultant tasting of sensual experience, and the need she expressed.

In the photographs Weston made of Tina during this year one can see why. "Tina hit Edward like a tempest; she had about her a magnificence and a nobility no one who knew her could ever afterward forget."[6] But in that early time of their relationship Weston has also caught her rapt gaze and youthful passion. When Tina talks about "the beauty which has been added to my life," it suggests that her love for Robo might have been unsatisfactory in some way, perhaps physically, and that their relationship, though not strained, was not as fulfilling as Tina had hoped. It also suggests an awareness of a change in her nature.

One might ask why it was Weston to whom Tina responded in so clear a way that the clandestine meetings were eagerly sought out by her, without any false modesty or reticence.

Edward Weston, today regarded as one of America's greatest photographers, in 1921 was thirty-five years old, married, and the father of four boys. He had been in California since 1906 and was living in Glendale, a suburb of Los Angeles. He had been both a commercial and professional photographer, but even his commercial portraits bore evidence of a greatness to come. He had already been awarded prizes in exhibitions, and his work had been acclaimed by critics and by other photographers. Imogen Cunningham, herself a marvelous photographer, had written words of high praise for his work in 1920.

Weston is described by a friend as "not an imposing man; he was small but powerfully built, nor was he, in fact, particularly handsome." Soft-voiced and gentle, he was nonetheless an extrovert. He had had very little formal education; "his remarkable and acute intelligence was simply directed another way."

Growing up in the Midwest, Weston had been raised by a sister and an aunt, his mother having died when he was only five years old. His addiction to photography started in 1902, when his father, a doctor, gave him a Bulls-Eye camera for his sixteenth birthday. Although he later worked for Marshall Field & Company in Chicago, with surveyors on railroads in Los Angeles and Nevada, as a house-to-house professional portrait photographer, he knew from the start the profound meaning that the art of photography held for him.

His marriage to Flora May Chandler, a close friend of his sister, was in many ways a throwback to his proper Midwest upbringing, and they had four sons. By 1921, when he met Tina, he had abandoned his commercial success and begun experimenting in photography. He had become increasingly discontent with the strictures of family life; his relationship with his wife had deteriorated over the years, and he had had numerous affairs. On the other hand, his relationship with his sons was constant and profound, a responsibility he eagerly accepted.

Weston's was a constant battle against poverty. He had to support himself, to support his belief in his art, and to contribute to the support of his family. His wife, a teacher, was the financial mainstay of the household. But Weston also pursued a separate existence, spending much of his time with his group—McGehee, Mather, and Johan Hagemeyer, another photographer— party-going, attending concerts, drinking wine and enjoying endless discussions.

Life in the Weston household in Glendale must have been madly inhibiting, and the atmosphere of Robo's studio provided a haven for him and his group. We wonder whether Robo's family had helped to contribute toward the security and comfort of Robo and Tina, since the meetings of friends there might have provided comradeship as well as a sense of well-being.

Why did Tina fall in love with Weston at this time of her life? She was twenty-five years old and involved in a conscious search for direction in her life. Hollywood provided no answer —it demeaned her intentions. She was unschooled but immensely curious about the intellectual world. Here was an older, more sophisticated man who had temperament and background so unlike her own—and probably unlike that of Robo (Weston often proclaimed himself to be 100 per cent American). He was a man who used sexuality as a means of self-expression and liberation, a man with a single-minded devotion to his art. He would allow neither himself nor his art to be betrayed by convention. His virility and physicality, which are generally acknowledged, must have electrified Tina. Although we have no evidence, we might assume Tina's sexual inexperience up to this time.

Robo's uncertainty and timidness about himself and about his work; Tina's disappointment with Hollywood and its disregard of her desire to act; probably her own searching and seeking a useful and creative life—all these factors must have contributed to her enchantment with Weston and his group. She wanted to share in their excursions, explorations, discussions. Her involvement with these people may have provided a kind of education pointing a way to the future. It is perhaps for this reason that she also sought the friendship of Johan Hagemeyer, one of Weston's closest friends. Hagemeyer had known Weston since 1917 and had shared his devotion to photography and music. On August 21, 1921, while visiting her family in San Francisco, Tina wrote to Hagemeyer:

> Before everything else, please excuse if I have misspelled your name as I fear I have. Mr. Weston gave me your address before leaving (or rather I asked him for it) as I was looking forward to see you. He also told me of the good books and music you have (therefore my impertinence). I am only going to be here one week more, so any time it is convenient for you, please call me on the phone and I will come over. My number is Franklin 9566—about 9 o'clock in the morning is the best time. Tina de Richéy.

On September 16, Weston wrote to Hagemeyer from Los Angeles: "Tina goes to Mexico very shortly—she wrote me and said 'I realized then how deep the friendship between J. H.

44

and you must be—for in him there was so much that made me think of you—and again you remind me much of him. Thanking him for the precious afternoon is not enough—I must also tell you how much I appreciated his cordial kindness and sympathetic company.'" Tina had obviously planned to go to Mexico to join Robo. There appears to have been no rupture in their marriage, the affair with Weston being sporadic and perhaps at that time more a manifestation of their restlessness, a purely physical experience rather than a commitment. Tina cherished the exposure to books and music which Hagemeyer provided and perhaps also unconsciously sought a physical and intellectual closeness to him as a surrogate for Weston.

She wrote again to Hagemeyer on September 17, from Los Angeles:

> I have written you about a dozen letters in my mind but never have I been able to put them into written form. Not for lack of thoughts—instead—the impressions left to me of the afternoon spent with you were so many and so deep they overwhelmed my mind. But here I am making a brave effort to express all I feel full well knowing it is futile—for not even to myself can I clearly answer why I suppressed the great desire I had to call on you once more. Was it power of will? or was it cowardice? Maybe the same spirit moved me then, what moved Oscar Wilde to write this paradox. "There are only two tragedies in this world; one consists in not obtaining that which you desire; the other consists in obtaining it." The last one is the worst—the last is a real tragedy. And so I left without satisfying my desire of listening once more to Pergolesi's

"Nina"* in your company. Since then I have played it twice—only twice—for I fear to play it oftener—and besides I must be alone when I listen to it—all alone— in order to give myself the illusion that I am not alone, nor here, but in 2616 Webster Street [Hagemeyer's old address]. Whether I will ever see you again or not, the brief but rich hours spent with you are most precious to me and I will live them over with the same beauty and sadness of that day. Thanking you for the joy your books and music together with your sympathetic company have procured me.

I have not seen your friend Edward since I returned, but he asked me to pose once more for him before leaving for Mexico. That made me very happy and filled me with pride. Oh! I hope he does something very great again! For his sake—as for me I cannot desire anything greater than what he has already done of me. Tina.

Several things, which we know only from Tina's writing, become evident in this correspondence. It is August 1921. The affair with Weston, having begun just four months ago, might appear to have been just an affair. Robo is still very much in the picture; he is not to leave until December of that year, and Tina has indicated that she plans to join him. This is not a spontaneous decision, but has been planned by both.

Weston had made his first photographs of Tina and was eager to continue. Tina was fascinated by Weston and revered his work. It is even possible that Weston had already started teaching Tina to use the camera. Maddow states that "she soon became his pupil, his model, his admirer, and his mistress:

---

*Giovanni Batista Pergolesi, eighteenth century composer.

Roubaix de L'Abrie Richéy (Robo), by Edward Weston. c.1921

Tina, California, by Edward Weston. 1921

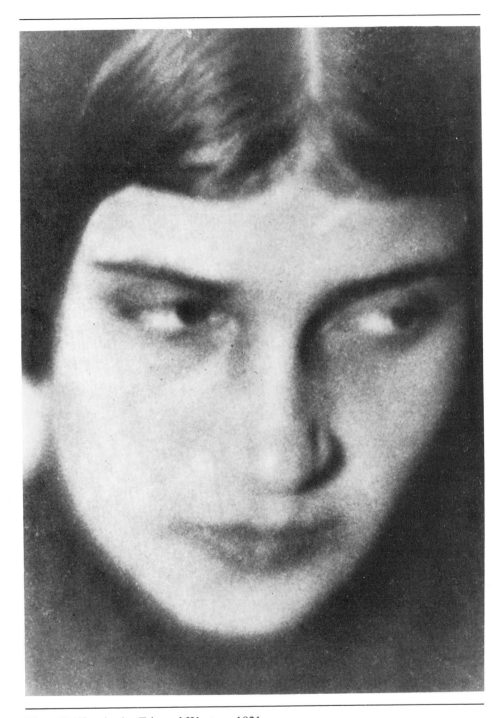

Tina, California, by Edward Weston. 1921

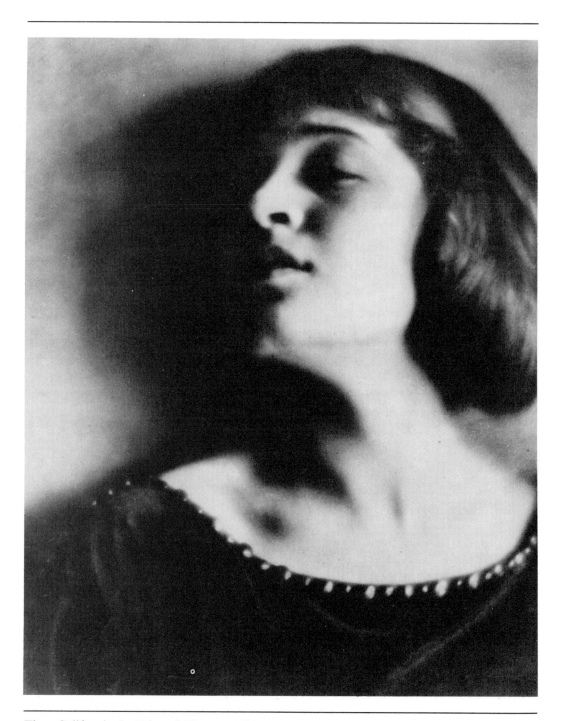

Tina, California, by Edward Weston. 1921

Tina, Los Angeles, by Edward Weston. c.1921

Assunta Modotti, Tina's mother, by Edward Weston. c.1922

Tina, Glendale, California, by Edward Weston. 1922

all three more or less at the same time."[7] For her their affair seems to have begun something that was more than a sexual adventure: Tina became aware of her own sexuality, and the possibilities of an independent future.

As we look at Weston's photographs of this period we see an extraordinarily beautiful woman, whose intense sexuality is perhaps heightened by her vulnerability. The photographs definitely belong to Weston's romantic period—the soft lens focusing on Tina's timid and youthful gaze, her face filled with the breath of love; they are more revealing of the sitter than were Weston's previous portraits. In her face are a subtlety and a hint of the dignity to come. The photograph illustrated on page 51 is one that is unknown to Weston's family and the historians of his art, but it must have had special meaning for Tina since it was in her possession up until her death and was used on her bier.

While there must also have been feelings of guilt on Weston's part because of his relationship with Tina, he and Robo remained friends. Two weeks after Robo arrived in Mexico, he wrote to Weston in glowing terms of this "land of extremes." He called it the artist's paradise, and said:

> There is little that is devoid of beauty. There is for me more poetry in one lone enshrouded figure leaning in the door of the pulque shop at twilight or a bronzen daughter of the Aztecs nursing her child in a church than could be found in Los Angeles in the next ten years . . . Can you imagine an art school where every-thing is free to everyone—Mexicans and foreigners alike—tuition, board, room, paint, canvas, models, all free—no entrance examination—if one will study,

that is the only requirement. After ten years of war and unrest it is wonderful to see what is being done here.

Robo described the landscape, the ancient cities and monuments, volcanos, and the many friends he had gained. He tried hard to persuade Weston to join him, and closed his letter, "Believe me to be as ever your friend, 'Robo.'" Robo became suddenly ill with smallpox, and after a brief but violent few days he died on February 9, 1922.

In a newspaper interview after his death and on the occasion of a posthumous exhibition of his paintings and batiks, some of which had been designed for her to wear in the movies, Tina stated: "We didn't even know it until toward the end. I was on a train going to him when I was handed a telegram—he was dead. I am thinking of him—dying alone, with no member of his family near him. It was terrible." He was thirty-one. In Tina's tribute to her husband she wrote, "Death came, swift and inexorable, and he vanished . . . from a world in which he did not belong."

Among the prose she selected for publication, Tina included Robo's "Words," in which he describes the personal significance which certain words have for him. To him "Robo is a rolling motion, as the waves in the ocean or the curved back of a brush"; "Tina is wine red and something very precious that one puts gently down to become more precious as they carefully put it down."

These words may indicate Robo's awareness that Tina was growing away from him toward Weston. He may reluctantly have acknowledged that he was destined to lose Tina. Did his knowledge of the affair hasten his decision to accept the invitation to go to Mexico and look for a "sympathy and romance"

Robo's mother at his grave in the Pantheon of Dolores, Mexico, D.F. 1922

that he could no longer find in Los Angeles? We know from Tina's family that there was no estrangement between them, and that she had planned to join him. But, unfortunately, we have no record of letters that they may have exchanged during that period.

Tina herself must have felt some guilt, not only because of the affair with Weston but probably because of the emotions and passions that it had awakened in her. While there had been no explicit bourgeois rules of behavior in her upbringing, it is probable that up to the time of Weston Tina had observed the moral code of marriage. For his part, Weston had had other loves and other sexual adventures before Tina.

A sense of family was always very strong in Tina, and this had evidently extended to Robo's family as well, particularly in her relationship with Robo's mother. Emily Edwards, a writer, remarks in a letter: "Once I met the delicately beautiful woman who had been Tina's mother-in-law . . . his [Robo's] mother and Tina seemed to be tenderly fond of one another. They are so very different. The slim conventional older woman seemed the younger of the two—an ageless maturity was Tina's." Tina and Robo's mother went together to Mexico after Robo's death, and it was in Mexico that Tina sensed the challenging possibilities for the expansion of her own self.

She stayed for several weeks, discovering the stirring times, the glowing landscape, renewing her friendship with Robelo and meeting the many friends Robo had made. She had also brought several of Weston's photographs and found a warm response from Mexican artists and intellectuals when she arranged for a showing in the *Academia de Bellas Artes*. His work was a revelation for the Mexican artists, who had previously given photography little attention as an art form.

Tina went to Mexico in 1922, a year which saw a great resurgence of national pride: "Mexico for the Mexicans." Anita Brenner describes this period:

> There was a lift, a stirring feeling in Mexico in the early twenties when the last chief had made his arrangements with Obrégon, and each agrarian cradled his gun in some safe place, like the roofhatch. It was new, it was a spring world where fear was skewered . . . there was a sense of strength released: much work to do, everything at the beginning . . . Artists returned from guerrilla trooping and from war-exhausted Europe; poets wrote lyrics, peasants humanized tractors with flowers and Indian nicknames for steam shovels.[8]

By 1921, President Obrégon had re-established a Ministry of Education with José Vasconcelos, who had returned from a five-year exile, as Minister. Vasconcelos was highly enthusiastic about the cultural aspects of the revolution, which would involve the contemporary artist in the life of the country. He held to the thesis that the Indian should be "redeemed" and the masses educated. He had been a friend of Zapata and one-time soldier with Pancho Villa. By providing them with commissions, Vasconcelos enabled the artists to serve to their fullest abilities and without ideological censorship.

It was this Mexico which Robo had glimpsed and which Tina now discovered for herself. Painters in overalls were putting the meaning of the revolution on public walls; they communicated with feeling and force what they had to say. Critics from all over the world felt that this was the first great modern art to have been created in America.

The birth of a Mexican school of painters whose inspiration came from the Mexican scene did not, however, occur overnight. Nor were the implications of this phenomenon confined to the sphere of artistic activity. "The stirrings of artistic revolt in Mexico preceded the political upheaval. In 1909, Dr. Atl, a pioneer figure in the history of Mexican art, had begun to preach nationalism. The following year, the students at the *Academia de Bellas Artes* (including the young David Alfaro Siqueiros) struck against the obsolete methods practiced here and walked out, never to return."[9]

Francisco Goítia and José Clemente Orozco were already independently pointing the way to social paintings. They were joined later by a large group of art students in a revolt against the Huerta dictatorship. By 1919 a congress of soldier-artists convened to plan new directions for art and for culture generally. David Alfaro Siqueiros and Carlos Orozco Romero were sent off to Europe for study; there, Siqueiros was to meet Diego Rivera. Their relationship was to have important repercussions for the developing arts in Mexico and for their own artistic developments.

Diego Rivera was in Paris during the important years of the Cubist period and was associated with Braque, Klee and Picasso. In Italy he was much impressed with the great frescoes, the Byzantine mural mosaics and the Etruscan relics that recalled to him the plastic strength of ancient Mexican art. He returned to Mexico in July 1921 to paint his first mural. David Alfaro Siqueiros had joined Carranza's revolutionary army in 1913, and was an active soldier until he left Mexico. While traveling in Europe, 1919–1922, he began to formulate his views on the artistic revolution, and he published a manifesto in Barcelona in May, 1921, stating for the first time his conception of monumental mural painting. Rivera and Siqueiros were to lead the Mexican artistic revolution and both were to figure largely in the life of Tina Modotti.

Together they organized the Revolutionary Syndicate of Technical Workers, Painters and Sculptors (*Sindicato de Técnicos, Pintores y Escultores*). Their publication, *El Machete*, became the medium for proclaiming their aims. Speaking to the Mexican people, they declared solidarity in the effort to overthrow the old, inhuman system and to recognize the spiritual vitality of the race. They sought to restore the peculiar ability of the Mexican to create beauty through indigenous Mexican art. "It is great because it surges from the people; it is collective, and our own aesthetic aim is to socialize artistic expression, to destroy bourgeois individualism . . . We hail the monumental expression of art because such art is public property." Such was the manifesto issued by the *Sindicato* in 1922 (the year of Tina's first visit to Mexico), the time of Obrégon's presidency and the beginning of a tremendous program in the arts. Cultural activity was encouraged through a broad program of popular education, renewed interest in the popular arts, open-air schools, (which Robo had reported glowingly in his letter to Weston).

The nationalistic movement in painting was leaving its mark on market places, government offices, churches and other public buildings. Mexican folk tunes and regional music and instruments came into fashion. Moreover, the renaissance was not limited to artistic activity. Women assumed a significant new place in society. They gained the right to vote and to participate in government and business. New educational opportunities, as well as co-education, became available to them.

Mexico was indeed for the Mexicans, but they also gave asylum to political exiles from Central and South American countries and offered them jobs with the encouragement that their lives might take root in Mexico. Tina did not find this Mexico alien to her. She was moved by all she saw and by the promise of a future, and was determined to find a place for herself in the new Mexico—the Mexico of the revolution. Upon her return to San Francisco after the death of her father, in March of 1922, she again sought to renew the friendship with Johan Hagemeyer. Tina had already begun, as Weston's pupil, to use the camera. And the fact that Hagemeyer was a photographer, an intellectual and an anarchist born in Europe must certainly have provided another bond in their friendship. She wrote to him shortly after her return, on April 7, 1922:

> I hesitated long whether to get in touch with you or not for I had made it my programme before coming here not to see anyone outside of my family. But the other day—finding myself alone—an uncontrollable desire came upon me to hear "Nina" again. And so I did—and as I listened to it the agitated life of these past few months became dimmer and dimmer while the memory of a certain afternoon came back to me with all the illusion of reality—a certain afternoon when for the first time that soul-torturing music took hold of me and left me a little sadder perhaps but with a richer soul. And because of all this I feel the desire to spend another afternoon with you—can the first ever be duplicated? I fear not—but "Nina" at least will be the same. Can you drop me a card and let me know when I can call? I

will remain here until Easter—fond as I am of this place—yet I am anxious to leave it—it holds too many memories for me—here I live constantly in the past, and "Life," said George Moore, "is beautiful at the moment, but sad when we look back." For me life is always sad—for even in the present moment I feel the past. Mine must be a spirit of decadence, and by living here I only give vent to it—but yet—I feel that only by living in the past can we revenge ourselves on nature—I wonder how you feel about all this—perhaps we can talk it over. Cordially, Tina Modotti de Richéy.

The loss of husband and father within a two-month period must have been shattering to Tina. She often came to San Francisco to see her family; she even thought about opening a photographic studio there. Hagemeyer might have provided a comforting friendship without the stress accompanying emotional and physical involvement.

The affair with Weston was continuing, although it was not without its trials and digressions. In early letters to Weston, Tina sounds as though she amazed herself with the deepness of her love and felt elated to give unstintingly, ready not only for the elemental sexuality of their relationship, but also for the beauty which it added to her life. She wrote to him in October 1922, when their relationship seemed to be floundering, "Good-bye—good-bye Edward, may you attain all you deserve—but is that possible—you give so much—how can 'Life' ever pay you back? I can only send a few rose petals and a kiss." (It was to be several months before Weston and Tina left for Mexico, where they started their lives together.) It sounds as though Tina felt that their affair was over, and in a letter to

Hagemeyer in October she asked if he had heard from Weston since his arrival in Ohio on a visit to his sister. Yet when Weston went to New York in November of that year, they obviously remained in touch. Weston noted in his Daybook (p. 10) that "Tina sent two 'specials,' each with $20 enclosed, knowing that I would need money; that I must see Balieff's 'Chauve Souris.' "

Weston's involvement with Tina had by this time extended to her family as well, and he was warmly welcomed into the household. Even after the death of Tina's father this warm, closely-knit group provided that sense of family which was so completely lacking in Weston's own experience. He made an exquisite portrait of Tina's mother, revealing the dignity and inner strength of the woman. Tina's younger sister Yolanda had started to work for him as a receptionist in 1922, and so the intimacy extended even outside the household. This relationship with Tina's family was to continue into the later years.

Tina, Mexico, by Edward Weston. Initialed and dated EW 1923

1923-1926
Mexico: The Legend of Tina and Weston

2 It is not certain what brought about Weston's decision to leave wife and family and go off with Tina on what Ben Maddow calls a "psychic voyage." Was it perhaps a new-found confidence in himself and his work, gained from his trip to New York, as well as the warm reception of his work in Mexico? It may have been the fear of losing Tina when she left the United States for Mexico. Or it may have been the endless pressures of his family life in Glendale. Whatever combined to stimulate him into action, Tina, Edward, and his eldest son Chandler, then thirteen years old, left for Mexico on July 30, 1923, on board the S.S. Colima. They left "after months of preparation, after such endless delays that the proposed adventure seemed but a conceit of the imagination, never actually to materialize."[1]

On board, Weston's jealousy manifested itself. "Thanks to

Tina—her beauty—though I might have wished it otherwise! El Capitan has favored us in many ways: the use of his deck, refreshing drinks in his cabin, his launch to carry us ashore."

Their first overland trips from the port city of Manzanillo and then by train to Colima and Guadalajara gave them glimpses of the beauty and sharp contrasts of the Mexican landscape. One thing pleased them—there were no questions either in hotels or apartments as to the personal relations of the travelers.

Finally Mexico City and their first house in Tacubaya, a suburb about forty minutes' trolley ride from the city. Weston describes it in a Daybook entry (p. 15). "We have leased an old and beautiful hacienda for six months; ten rooms, each opening onto a spacious patio, 85 × 100, with high ceilings and tall arched windows, barred, heavily shuttered, seeming to suggest possible attack . . . the brick walls of our casa are fifteen inches thick and plastered in and out . . . ." They both enjoyed shopping and bargaining in the rambling market; Tina's familiarity with the language (she spoke Spanish with an Italian lilt) made these occasions both profitable and enjoyable. They bargained for everything and bought the Indian wares and food, as well as the bizarre objects sold in the market place. From their roof they could see the snow-capped volcanoes, Ixtacihuatl and Popocatepetl, and even sometimes the spires of the cathedral in Mexico City.

Unlike many other Americans, who came to "attend" a revolution, or to study the Aztec and the Mayan, and who tended to befriend fashionable intellectuals, Weston and Tina associated with artists and revolutionists. From the beginning they were not without friends in Mexico. Tina had already met many artists and intellectuals through Gómez Robelo.

She was eager for Edward to meet them and see their work, as well as to have them know Weston's photographs. They met the painters, the poets, the writers. Tina renewed her acquaintance with Xavier Guerrero, then a young painter working with Diego Rivera; his sister Elisa; Jean Charlot, the painter and writer who had been in Mexico since 1921; José Vasconcelos, the guiding spirit behind the painted walls; and the poet Juan de la Cabada. She had originally met Guerrero in 1923, when he brought a folk art exhibition to Los Angeles. We can see the majesty and beauty of that man in one of Tina's great photographs. They were to share a long and deep relationship after Weston left Mexico and up until Guerrero left for the Soviet Union in 1928.

Unfortunately, the stay in Tacubaya was very short-lived. They were obliged to move because no telephone service was available in the outlying districts and a telephone seemed essential to their livelihood. After much house-hunting (little could compare to the charm of their hacienda), they found a house on Calle Lucerna in the Colonia Juárez. This location gave them more opportunities to explore Mexico City.

There was furious activity in the city in that year. The streets were full of tram-cars and *camiones* rushing about; vendors of *pulque*, sweets, fruits and foods, toys and lacquerware were offering their wares. And music—*mariachi* bands on the streets singing for themselves and for the revolution amid the flower vendors offering their almost overpowering fragrances for *centavos*. The acrid smoke of cooking fires mingled with pungent spices. The *Zócalo* (Plaza) was dominated by the Mexican Cathedral, that imposing mixture of architectural styles ranging from that of the Spanish *conquistadores* to the baroque.

Across a broad open expanse was the National Palace and other public buildings. The *Zócalo* was also the scene of other kinds of activity. Within the buildings, artists were at work in overalls just like the masons who were working with them (at the same wage scale). Mexicans were arriving in groups to petition for their rights, to ask for schools, or water for the pueblos, or simply to observe and enjoy their capital and their heritage.

This activity extended to areas outside the city. Teachers were carrying books from door to door; art became so popular that open-air art schools for children were founded; painters were telling the story of Mexico and archaeologists and anthropologists were digging the great ruined pyramids and temples to discover the past so that the Indian and the *mestizo* could take their proper place as the foundation for the modern society.

A day's outing took Tina and Weston to Xochimilco, filled with asphalt and stone roads leading to floating islands of flowers and vegetables and slender willows divided by canals. All this reminded Tina of Italy, as did the sunshine, the colors, the gaiety of the people. They went to bullfights (to the pageantry of which only Weston responded) and on other excursions into the countryside, participating in the local fiestas to which they were constantly invited.

On the occasion of Weston's first exhibition, at "Aztec Land," a tourist shop in the center of the city, Diego Rivera, together with his wife Guadalupe, responded to Weston's work with "a quiet, keen enjoyment." Thus began a long, not quite smooth friendship, with Diego and Lupe visiting Calle Lucerna, and Weston and Tina joining the festivities at the

Tina (4th from left) and Weston in the Marín family home, Guadalajara, Mexico. 1924

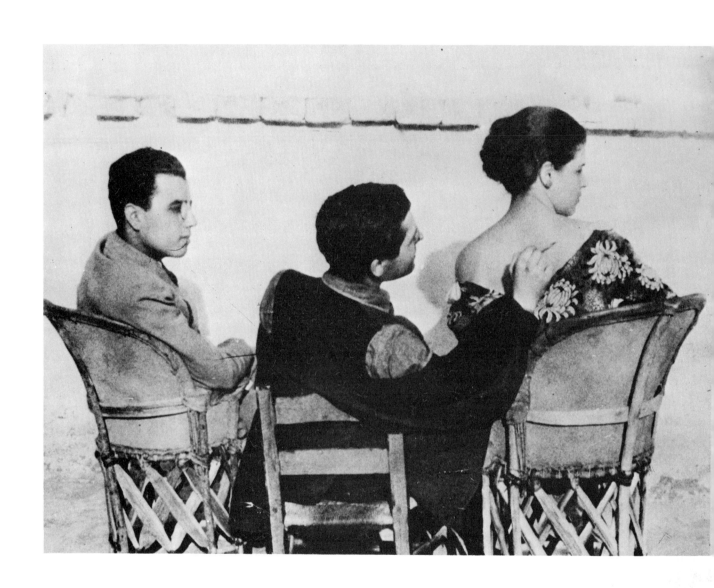

Left to right: Federico Marín, Jean Charlot, Tina Modotti, on the *azotea*, by Edward Weston. 1924

Rivera household. Lupe was mercurial in her reactions to Tina—sometimes accusing Diego of having an affair with Tina, and at times penitent for her suspicions about Tina. She was never to believe that nothing existed between them. As recently as December, 1971, in a newspaper interview in *Excelsior*, she said, "Diego was not a womanizer, but the women followed him very much. He began to visit a young Italian, and although he denied that they were having an affair, I did not believe him, and our situation was becoming more and more difficult; finally one day, he confessed that it was true; that he was having an affair with Modotti." Diego himself had said that it was in part his friendship with Tina which helped move Lupe toward a divorce.[2]

The parties which Tina and Weston had in their home became weekly reunions with much gaiety, singing, dancing, food and drink. Federico Marín, Lupe's younger brother, and Carlos and María Orozco Romero (he the painter and she the sister of Lupe) tell of one occasion when they were all together and Tina had prepared an excellent spaghetti with butter and cheese —the Neapolitan way. Federico describes Tina as "a mysterious beauty, without any vulgarity, very polite and introverted. She was always taking care of everything and spreading happiness all around her." An inquiry as to whether she was a merry person brought this response from him: "No—austere— terribly austere; not melancholy, neither sad nor tragic. Many men fell in love with her, they even committed suicide, but it wasn't her fault." Carlos Orozco Romero confirmed this and Maria remembers her as "a real woman—it's the only thing I can say because she was good in the home and good at her artistic activities."

It seems evident (at least from the Daybooks) that both Tina and Weston enjoyed other loves during this period in Mexico. Tina was characterized by some as a "femme fatale" and dangerous for men. Like so many beautiful women, she had enormous sexual attraction for many men who desired her (an aspiring artist, rebuffed, once said that he wished Tina would kill him), but the nature of her relationship to several of those whose friendships she valued was unique. They were not casual infidelities. They were not simply the satisfactions of ego, of sex, or the expression of revenge and jealousies against Weston's sexual forays. That he resented her affairs is known, and he had said, "Next time I'll pick a mistress ugly as hell." He had indicated in his Daybook (p. 58), "There is a certain inevitable sadness in the life of a much-sought-for, beautiful woman, one like Tina especially, who, not caring sufficiently for associates among her own sex, craves comraderie and friendship from men as well as sex love . . . ." He certainly sounds as though he resents Tina for her pursuit of separate friendships—with or without sexual love—and it seems that he underestimated her ability to give and receive friendship among the women she knew. Anita Brenner tells of this period.

> We met sometime in 1923—in the weekly gatherings we were groups of painters and writers. We were all eventually close friends; we were sort of looking for the same things, working in the same channels. And it was not like the social friendships of now; it was a revolutionary atmosphere, almost like a workshop atmosphere, so we could all get into each other's "thing." I liked Tina very much; she was very warm and basically a very gentle person. Very romantic and, in a way,

clearer about where she was going (although she didn't know for sure) than Weston.

When asked about the rumors that Tina was considered promiscuous, Anita Brenner answered quite emphatically,

No! It was a romantic time in a way and it was a time of cutting loose and of making over the whole artistic world, both the European breakthroughs, the world breakthroughs and the Mexican breakthroughs were coming at the same time. Tina was not a conventional person; she lived with Weston, but it was the same as marriage. There were the same relationships of caring and working together. She did have other lovers from time to time which I think Weston knew about, but I think he did the same thing.

It is not difficult to assume that Tina, like so many women at that time, was making clear her disdain of bourgeois morality and affirming a single standard in her relationships.

Anita Brenner continues, "Basically she was an artist, and she was learning to photograph from Weston when I first met her. She was doing work in his darkroom and helping to finish his work."

Tina was starting to work on her own, and in Brenner's opinion what she did was in an entirely different mood. "It was much softer and more emotional—Weston was working towards sharpness and an architectural feeling and texture. Tina had a feeling for people and for all the romantic things that would come out of an Italian background."

Tina and Weston visited museums and private collections which revealed to them the qualities and depths of the ancient Mexican civilizations. They could understand so much better the work of the artists filling Mexican walls with the Mexican past. They broadened their social group to include politicos and other foreigners in Mexico. Among the latter group were some Americans—Carleton Beals, writer and critic, Ella and Bertram Wolfe, then both teachers. They traveled to Tepotzotlán, where the baroque architecture, rolling hills and the maguey enchanted them and where they both made photographs. Tina made her most interesting abstraction of the tower of Tepotzotlán (see p. 119). "She is very happy over it and well she may be. I myself would be pleased to have done it," Weston had stated.

The distractions of their social life, their separate affairs and their work kept them somewhat apart. By the end of January 1924 Weston wrote: "The night before we had been alone—so seldom it happens now. She called me to her room and our lips met for the first time since New Year's Eve. Then the doorbell rang—Chandler and a friend—our mood was gone." Yet they found time to sit together on their roof (*azotea*), reading aloud, discussing books, Tina recalling memories of Italy. And talking about their own love, which Tina expressed so beautifully on Weston's birthday in a letter, "a note of two words and three purple hyacinth buds" which conveyed more in simple emotion than pages could have done. The only words were: "Edward, Edward!" A single cry of many emotions: love, passion, anguish, tenderness.

Tina was able to make all kinds of lasting friendships, among them with Pablo O'Higgins, an American painter born in San Francisco, who had come to Mexico in 1924 and become an assistant to Rivera. O'Higgins has recalled the first time he met Tina:

Tina and Weston: their "anniversary" photograph, Mexico. 1924

I think it was one of the moments when Tina came to the *Secretaría de Educación* to take photographs, because Diego was very interested in Tina's photographing the work in progress so that you would see a piece of detail and the drawing on the plaster—to see at the base of things, as Diego called it. That's where I first saw Tina. Naturally, I was just another person, but she impressed me immediately as a beautiful woman. I mean beautiful—not trying to be beautiful—but born beautiful. Very much of Tina was always like that —never pretending to be anything she wasn't. Very open and frank. I told her that I would like to see some of her work and she invited me to where they were staying . . . she was living with Weston on Calle Lucerna, and so when I went there to see Tina, I met Weston too. We talked of many things and the next time I went I made a sketch of Tina that I liked very much because I liked the way she was sitting.

Rivera and Charlot also made fine drawings of Tina at this time (pp. 79, 83).

By May of 1924 Tina and Weston had to move again, this time to Avenida Vera Cruz. One of the Mexican women who came to sit for Weston at this time has said, "I keep a very good souvenir of her (Tina's) charm and personality—she used blue gins [sic] that were very unusual for women at this time." They continued their exploration of Mexico City, roaming the old streets and enjoying the bustling activity, visiting old, out-of-the-way churches. On one such day they calmly ventured into a photographer's studio and announced themselves as a wedded couple celebrating their first wedding anniversary.

They wanted a photograph to commemorate their anniversary. The postures and background were carefully planned by the photographer, while Tina and Weston obediently kept the pose and managed to strike a serious attitude (was it all play-acting?) (p. 75). It would appear that both were dressed in fairly conventional clothes. Tina, it seemed, always dressed as herself, not in a costume arranged to fit her into a particular role. She was a small woman, and almost always dressed in dark blue or black, preferably in skirts and blouses when she didn't wear the blue jeans. Of course, there were the Mardi Gras parties with funny masks and costumes, and Tina and Weston loved to change clothes on these occasions. Even with their exciting social life and their travels, Tina was to pose time and time again for Weston. Once she read poetry so that he could "attempt the registration of her remarkably mobile face in action"[3] (see p. 94).

Tina had been going off on her own using her camera to record the circus, puppet shows, churches, plazas, as well as the frescoes of Rivera. She worked in the darkroom on her own negatives, helping Weston with his, and also printing from old negatives by unknown photographers for Anita Brenner's book. She had her first public showing that year in the Palacio de Minerva, together with Weston and other artists. Weston was to comment, "Tina's lose nothing by comparison with mine—they are her own expression."[4]

Somehow the political scene—whether in the informal discussions at their weekly reunions, the meetings they attended, or the activities of friends whose lives were completely devoted to the revolution—was always present in their lives.

In spite of Weston's repeated success with his work in

Mexico, his concern and anxiety for his family back in Glendale caused him to leave Mexico after eighteen months of separation from his other boys. In December 1924, before he left, Tina wrote a note to him (out of respect for the other's privacy, they oftened exchanged written messages within the household): "What is the use of words between Edward and I? He knows me and I know him and we both have faith in each other. And that to me, Edward, seems the most precious gain we have acquired from each other—the faith in each other. I will be a good girl while you are gone Edward—I will work hard and that for two reasons—that you may be proud of me and that the time of our separation may move more swiftly. Edward—beloved—thank you—whatever comes." They spent hours before his departure trying to reconcile their lives, and Tina claimed that her mind was clearly focused—"I want to go with you Edward, to be your 'apprentice' and work in photography." Chandler, on the other hand, wanted to remain and Tina had offered to care for him but he left with his father at the end of December 1924.

Weston was to return to Mexico but Tina wrote him frequently, often confessing (July 7, 1925): "I have not been very 'creative,' Edward—less than a print a month—that is terrible! And yet it is not lack of interest so much as lack of discipline and power of execution . . . speaking of my personal self—I cannot—as you once proposed to me—solve the problem of life by losing myself in the problem of art—not only I cannot do that but I even feel that the problem of life hinders my problem of art."

Here perhaps are the first stirrings of realizations of the incompatibility of her life and her art: to be with Weston, to be

Drawing of Tina by Jean Charlot. 1924

Drawing of Tina by Pablo O'Higgins. 1924

his apprentice, conflicted with her growing consciousness in the atmosphere of social responsibility. We must remember that Tina, born in Italy and raised in poverty, was strongly influenced by the views of her proletarian father. At this time the memories of her youth must have been reawakened by her surroundings, providing still another link in her own development, and producing a strong kinship with the Mexican people and their problems. We can also assume that the ambience in Los Angeles with Robo's family was entirely bourgeois. And certainly Weston and the group which met in Robo's studio were, in effect, bourgeois-turned-bohemian-and-radical (though not politically)—Tina being probably the only true proletarian among them. At the same time, she was posing for Diego Rivera's murals in the Chapel at the Chapingo Agricultural School, "Virgin Earth" and "Germination." These daily contacts brought her into the company of a dedicated political person who, while not consciously proselytizing, must have expressed his views to her and educated her about another way of life.

Weston was at this time not simply apolitical but outspokenly anti-Communist. In their personal relationship he held out little hope for their lives together. One wonders if they ever discussed the possibilities of his divorce from Flora and their eventual marriage, or if there was some unspoken understanding that this was impossible.

Tina was still on a search for her own identity. She was certainly aware of the conflicts within her, but her personal independence and instinctive identification with political struggle was not to be resolved until she made personal commitments to a politically active role. And too, with Weston gone, she may have yearned for another emotional involvement in her life which would help point the way to some clarification of the future.

In August 1925, after an absence of eight months, Weston returned to Mexico. This time he was accompanied by his second eldest son, fourteen-year-old Brett. When they arrived in Guadalajara, Tina and Elisa Guerrero, sister to Xavier, were at the station platform to meet them. They spent ten days there, during which time Weston's and Tina's work was shown in Guadalajara's *Museo del Estado*. They had happy reunions with the Marín family, whose home was always open to them. Returning to Mexico City, their lives resumed the old pattern: parties, dances, excursions, sittings, visits from Tina's sister Mercedes, John Dewey, René d'Harnoncourt. Life in the household went on as before until it was interrupted by Tina's departure for San Francisco to visit her mother, who was seriously ill. Weston noted that "the house seemed so strangely empty." He appears to have been ambivalent in his feelings toward Tina at this time, resenting her lovers, though he doesn't name any one specifically except for a Dr. M who just wanted to worship her. At the same time he felt no pressure in Tina's love for him since there was never any indication of the possessiveness of "a woman madly in love." And he freely "romped" with the servants in the household and pursued Xavier's sister at the same time.

In San Francisco on January 25, Tina wrote:

Eduardito, a letter from you today. How I look forward to those long, cream-colored envelopes. When one is handed to me a thrill goes over my whole body. Things have been very chaotic and difficult with me

Drawing of Tina by Diego Rivera. 1926

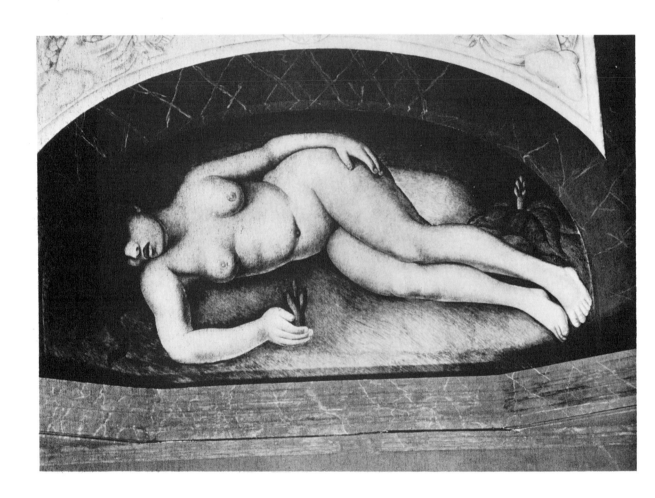

"Virgin Earth," detail of mural by Diego Rivera in Chapingo Agricultural School, Mexico. 1925

Detail of mural by José Clemente Orozco, National Preparatory School, Mexico, 1926. Photograph by Tina Modotti, 1928

but Consuelo [Kanaga—a photographer friend from Mexico] has done much to help me. Today Dan took me all around to camera dealers in search of a second-hand Graflex and trying to sell my Corona—dear little Corona—I feel so attached to it but you won't think me ungrateful for trying to sell it? I explained in my last letter the reason and I can't get one without selling the other. There is much I want to talk to you about—all my impressions of the U.S.—all my reactions—all my ideas of working differently in photography when I return . . . . little mamacita is feeling fine these days—oh, what a relief for us! We pet her and spoil her to death—her regards to you—she and everybody here also loves you—your name is always mentioned in connection with something nice . . .

In a later letter she confides a feeling of helplessness—

When it comes to doing things for myself I just feel impotent—I don't know which way to start or turn—you know what they say about a prophet in one's own country. Well, in a way it works for me too—you see—this might be called my home town—well, of all the friends and acquaintances not one takes me seriously as a photographer—not one has asked me to show my work— only the ones I met through you . . . . I am going to work hard when I return to Mexico and differently—if I can get a Graflex—I have always been too restrained in my work *as you well know* but I feel now with a Graflex I will be able to loosen up . . . . This is all for now dear, short but hardly sweet because I feel rather gloomy . . . but it is only temporary so—don't worry—rather forgive me—it seems so long, so long since I have been near you and talked with you—I miss you dear . . .

Imogen Cunningham, a friend of Weston's, had met Tina on the occasion of her visit to San Francisco and she and her then-husband Roi Partridge purchased the photograph of the wine glasses. Cunningham recalls, "to me she was a performer of real interest . . . I was never critical of her, never noticed her accent if she had one, just took in her beauty."

Tina's feelings of impotence and helplessness at this time may be an expression of feeling alien in the ambience of the United States where indeed she was less at home than in Mexico in the household she shared with Weston. It is not surprising that she felt that Mexico was "home" (this in spite of the seeming frivolity of Weston's and her separate sexual encounters). She could communicate with him, with her close friends, and share with them the seriousness of their professional and social concerns in light of the political climate there.

These were perilous days in Mexico. Plutarco Elías Calles, a member of the Obrégon cabinet, had been President since the end of 1924. He had strong support from Luis Morones, a labor boss with a tight political machine, who had become his Minister of Labor, thus allowing Calles to proclaim his a labor government. The Federation of Unions, known as CROM—the Revolutionary Federation of Mexican Labor—worked hand in hand with the government; almost all other unions outside of CROM were broken. There seemed to be some progress: roads were built—a series of dams—schools and hospitals—there was a business boom but with little more than lip service to the demands of the revolution. While work on the new constitution continued, it produced little against the oil interests and the power of the church; land distribution programs had slowed down to a halt. The Church conflict grew with a decree that the priesthood would be under government control. The Church denounced the decree and supported guerrillas called *Cristeros*, who spread propaganda, raided the rural schools and murdered the teachers.

At this time too relations were strained with the United States because of potential dangers to the oil and land interests and because of Mexico's support of the Nicaraguan resistance to the U.S. Marines. Tina had worked with the Hands-off Nicaragua Committee in Mexico (see p. 164).

In March of 1926, Tina and Weston again exhibited together, billed as "The Emperor of Photography—the *bellísima* Tina Modotti—an irresistible combination." This reference to Tina as "the beautiful Tina Modotti" surely displeased her. Therefore the review of the exhibition by Diego Rivera must have struck a welcome note: "Tina Modotti has done marvels in sensibility on a plane, perhaps more abstract, more aerial, even more intellectual, as is natural for an Italian temperament. Her work flowers perfectly in Mexico and harmonizes with our passion."[5]

They continued their excursions out of the capital and both were excited by Anita Brenner's proposal for a project to record the art, architecture and crafts of Mexico. They went off to Puebla, Oaxaca, Michoacán, Jalisco, Guanajuato and Querétaro. Brenner was writing her now famous book, *Idols Behind Altars*, for which Weston and Tina had already made the photographs, and had in mind a further exploration of the past of Mexico through its art.

Often Tina worked alone and sometimes together with Weston in recording the works. Given the unsettled times, they were happy to leave Mexico City and the uneasiness there. Many of their friends were now scattered. In Michoacán they learned with horror of the death of their great friend, Manuel Hernández Galván, then a Senator, who was killed by political opponents. They were concerned about the fate of their other friends. They were becoming weary of travel week after week in areas where the rainy season inhibited work and made living uncomfortable. They kept seeing posters of the now-dead Galván as they moved into new towns. Finally they returned to Mexico City at least satisfied with the work accomplished.

But the home they shared in Mexico had changed. There were still visitors streaming in and out, and they all went to parties with their friends. But the legend of Tina and Edward was on the wane. Each was pursuing a different path. Weston was trying to have an affair with a woman he identified only as M., and Tina may already have begun her involvement with Xavier Guerrero. This was no ordinary rift, not just the cooling of fervor: Weston was finished with Mexico and impatient to be reunited with his other sons. Brett, who was beginning to produce photographs which delighted Weston, also was eager to return to the United States. In November they left, and Weston wrote in his Daybook: "The leaving of Mexico will be remembered for the leaving of Tina. The barrier between us was for the moment broken. Not till we were on the Paseo in a taxi rushing for the train did I allow myself to see her eyes. But when I did and saw what they had to say, I took her to me . . . Tina with tear-filled eyes. This time, Mexico, it must be adios forever. And you, Tina? I feel it must be farewell forever too."

Were Tina's tear-filled eyes a sign of bleak despair as another phase in her life had ended? There appears to have been no discussion about the possibility of Tina's leaving with Weston. Tina had made her decision to remain in Mexico, to pursue her own life and work there. She also at this time appears to have had firm convictions about her revolutionary feminism, which did not wait to be liberated but which she pursued in every aspect of her life. Remarriage—to Weston or anyone else—was of no interest to her.

The relationships that Tina shared with women contradict still another myth that even Weston helped to create: that Tina, like many beautiful women, did not care sufficiently for associates among her own sex. The words of Anita Brenner, María Marín de Orozco (Lupe Rivera's sister) and Emily Edwards seem to indicate a warm response to her.

Pablo O'Higgins had introduced Emily Edwards to Tina in 1926, shortly before Weston and Brett were to leave Mexico. Miss Edwards recalls:

> At that time, Tina, Edward Weston and his young son were together in Mexico City. I remember seeing a series of photos of her head, taken while she was talking; the tragedy she expressed astonished me.

> Tina always seemed to be the same person; whether as woman, artist or revolutionist—all-of-a-piece, as she lived simply what she was. Basically, she was beautiful. Her studio was always in simple good order, and this easy efficiency was in whatever she was doing. I was outside her revolutionary activities, but attended one meeting where she was in charge; and quiet efficiency ruled.

Tina was naturally generous and sensitive to others, but she did not tolerate intrusion nor was she unaware of the failings of her friends. Certainly she was unconventional, but she was shocked by vulgarity and presumption. She had her friendships of convenience but knew what she was doing. Tina had many different kinds of friends.

I was deeply in her debt for generous friendship and as you can see I both loved and trusted her.

Although she never had a child, Tina nevertheless had great affinities with young people. We can feel her response to the children of Mexico in her photographs, and sense her emotions in what she captured in their expressive eyes. She had, after all, cared for the younger children in her own family, who also had been hungry and sad. She had spent a good deal of time under the same roof with first Chandler and then Brett, and felt deeply for Weston's boys and his relationship with them. The Sunday morning after their departure, she was to write:

> Edward; I woke up with the nice feeling that you were here—My first thought was, I wonder if Edward is up yet?—but the illusion did not last long—and the vision of your and Brett's empty rooms hurt me as much as yesterday after my return here—I want to write you at length Edward—but not now—I cannot see now—
>
> You know that poem of Ezra Pound on page 172*—You are *that* to me Edward—No matter what others mean to me *you* are *that*—only you were embittered and had lost faith in me—but I never did because I

---

* *Modern American and British Poetry*, edited by Louis Untermeyer, has Pound's *Canto LXXXI* on p. 172. It begins:

What thou lovest well remains,
               the rest is dross
What thou lov'st well shall not be reft from thee

What thou lov'st well is thy true heritage
Whose world, or mine or theirs,
                  or is it of none?

Tina on the *azotea*, Mexico, by Edward Weston. c.1924

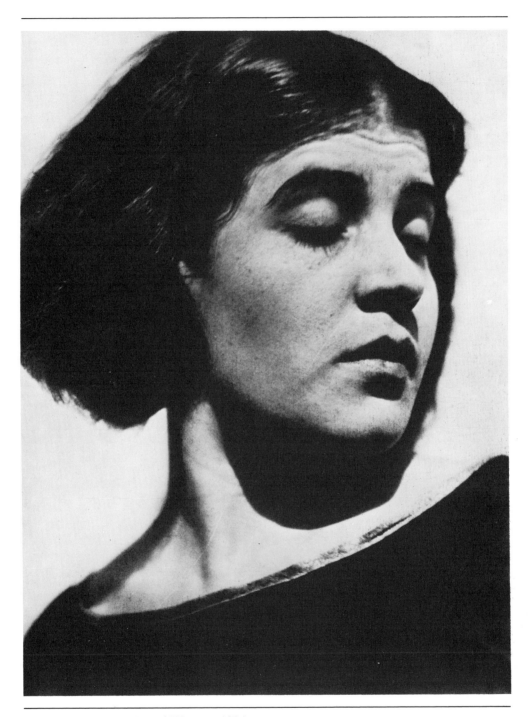

Tina, Mexico, by Edward Weston. 1924

Tina, Mexico, by Edward Weston. 1925

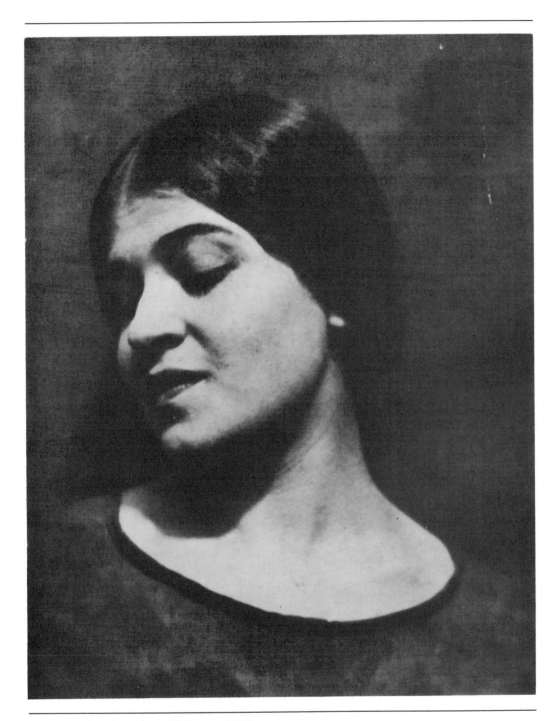

Tina, Mexico, by Edward Weston. 1925

respect the manifold possibilities of being found in all of us and also because I accept the tragic conflict between life which continually changes and form which fixes it immutable—

But I cannot write more—this terrible gnawing at my heart won't let me. Till soon dear—you are on the train now but when this reaches you, you will be surrounded by all your boys—I keep visualizing the picture of you with your boys for it brings a smile of great tenderness and peace on my lips—

The legend of Tina and Weston was over. She had now come to another crisis—another turning point in her life. She was thirty years old—once married—she had experienced the death of a husband and father—she had physically and spiritually left the United States (had she ever felt a kinship with it?)—she had had three years of a relationship which seemingly had been fulfilling in all its aspects. By all accounts, Tina was an honest person—honest in her relationship and honest to herself. Weston's departure was not precipitous, nor did their separation come as a surprise to her. It was probably not bleak despair that caused her tear-filled eyes but the realization that, whatever her passionate attachment to Weston had been, that aspect of their relationship was over. In all probability she had already become deeply involved with Xavier Guerrero. Her fundamental independence could be seen in her own view of the world, and in her future, which of necessity was also the rupture with Weston.

"The tragic conflict between life which continually changes and form which fixes it immutable" was probably the recognition deep within herself that the barrier between Weston and herself was unbridgeable—each had to go along consciously chosen paths, separate though they might be. And Tina must have cherished what remained for them to share—a rare and close communication.

There is a special tone in Tina's letters to Weston from this time onward. She never admonishes him for having abandoned her and their life in Mexico, but continually expresses a warmth and depth of friendship shared. Weston too in retrospect recognized what he called "the fineness of our association," and this quality surely made possible their closeness through letters.

Calla lilies, by Tina Modotti. c.1927

1926-1930
Mexico: Commitment to Revolution; Expulsion

3 Tina found her way into the life stream of Mexico. Passionate woman that she was, she poured her emotions into politics, identifying herself with Mexico's struggles and aspirations. From this point onward it was not difficult for her to align herself with Guerrero and with the Communist cause.

Xavier and Tina had met briefly in Los Angeles in 1923 and resumed their acquaintance on her arrival in Mexico. He had been working with Siqueiros and Rivera on the newspaper *El Machete* since 1922 and collaborated with Rivera on the frescoes in Chapingo. Although his art had involved him from youth with revolutionary Mexico, he became a political activist, living and working through the Communist Party in the service of world revolution. He undoubtedly saw a good deal of Tina during the period when Weston was in Mexico, and perhaps even before Weston's departure the relationship of Tina and Xavier had developed into more than friendship. This might have provided a sense of security at this point of Tina's life, not out of a sense of loneliness after the final break with Weston, but more through a sense of identification with a cause. She became a member of the Communist Party in 1927. She and Xavier, as artists, were able to share the same aesthetic concerns as well as their own place in the revolutionary struggle.

It has been suggested that Tina's association with the artists made her turn to Communism. Surely it contributed to her formalizing her position at this time, but we must also remember her early childhood sufferings and deprivations. Her own experiences in factories were still deep in her consciousness.

The photographs which Tina and Weston made in Mexico show very clearly the differences in their response to Mexico. Weston's truth is most visible in the individuals to whom he responded and whose portraits are revelations of sitter and photographer, particularly those he made of Tina, Diego Rivera, Lupe Marín, D. H. Lawrence. "He felt strongly the impact of the face itself, the head as a sculptured object, within which the springs of hate and love continually wound and unwound . . . an explosion of character itself."[1] Tina's photographs show a development of her style in relation to what was at the center of her being: the ordinary people she had observed, the tools, the burdens of life exalting her chosen subjects with a touch of poetry. She was able to make visible the humility, simplicity, solitude and fortitude of the Mexican people. She communicated her feelings about them with a

100

poignancy that is unforgettable. Tina had a quiet comprehension of all suffering.

It is apparent from available letters that Tina wrote relatively little about her own work to Weston. Occasionally she would send him a print of one of her favorites, like the Calla lilies (see p. 98). She hardly ever wrote all the details of her deepening political involvements, although she did write enough to indicate her commitments and those of their mutual friends. She remained devoted to Weston's development as an artist, bringing his new work to the attention of people who opinion both cared about. She would report these faithfully to him.

Tina also ardently expressed her own reactions to his work, and those reactions continued to be of importance to Weston. She remarks in one very important letter: "My God, Edward, your last photographs surely took my breath away. I feel speechless in front of them . . . " (July 25, 1927). She continues,

Edward—nothing before in art has affected me like these photographs—I just cannot look at them a long while without feeling exceedingly perturbed—they disturb me not only mentally, but physically—there is something so pure and at the same time so perverse about them—they contain both the innocence of natural things and the morbidity of a sophisticated, distorted mind—They make me think of lilies and of embryos at the same time—they are mystical and erotic.

She was referring to the series of shell photographs which Weston started to do in June 1927 and which were astonishing revelations of the purity and monumentality of natural forms—work truly unlike anything ever done in photography before.

Yolanda Modotti, Tina's sister;
by Tina Modotti. San Francisco. 1925

Federico Marín, by Tina Modotti. 1924

Benvenuto Modotti, Tina's brother;
by Tina Modotti. San Francisco. 1925

Anita Brenner, Mexico, by Tina Modotti. 1925

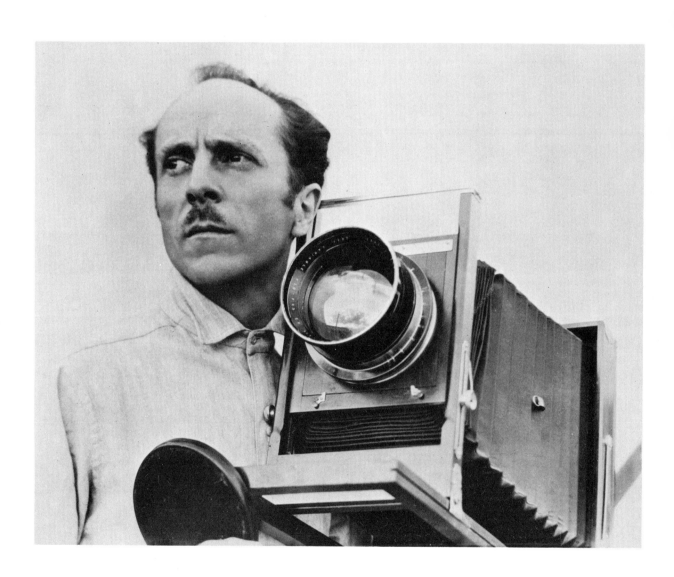

Edward Weston with his Graflex camera, Mexico, by Tina Modotti. 1923

Xavier Guerrero, Mexico, by Tina Modotti. c.1926

Dolores del Río, Mexico, by Tina Modotti. 1925

María Marín de Orozco, Mexico, by Tina Modotti. 1925

Although not all of Tina's letters to Weston were consulted, and his to her have vanished, we can assume that theirs was a steady exchange of correspondence. Their letters appear to have been numbered, so that if one number did not appear they would be aware of even the slightest discontinuity in their communication.

In 1927 Tina was to meet a man deeply involved in the political struggle of the times who was later to become her political mentor and, in the thirties, her companion. He was also an Italian; he came from Trieste, an area very like that of Udine. A committed anti-Fascist, he had known years of revolutionary activity in Italy as well as in the United States. It was perhaps this man, Vittorio Vidali, who rekindled in Tina the consciousness of her Italian heritage and the passion to return to Italy. He, like other radicals and liberals, had rallied to the defense of Nicola Sacco, a shoe-factory worker, and Bartolomeo Vanzetti, a fish peddler, who were convicted in 1921 of the murder of a Massachusetts paymaster and his guard.

The United States from the middle of the twenties onward was affected by hysterical mistrust of atheists, anarchists, aliens, and socialists and liberals in the trade union movements. Both Sacco and Vanzetti were anarchists, both were aliens who had evaded the army draft. Neither had a criminal record, nor did they have any of the money which was supposed to have been stolen from the paymaster. They were tried in the summer of 1921, convicted, and sentenced to death. From that time onward, the cause of Sacco and Vanzetti became the cause of liberals and radicals. Poets responded to the gentleness of the two humble Italians who were guilty only of a deep sincerity in their anarchistic political philosophy; painters were deeply moved by the contrast between the strength and integrity of the prisoners and the self-righteousness of the prosecution and their relentless pursuit of the mock trial. Protest meetings were held all over the United States, in Europe, and throughout Latin America. Just two months before Sacco and Vanzetti were to be electrocuted in 1927, Vittorio Vidali was deported from the United States and went to Mexico. He attended an important demonstration in June of that year for Sacco and Vanzetti and it was there that he first met Tina Modotti. Vidali was a challenging combination of physical and intellectual strength. He was a monolithic composition in which all of the pieces fell together: a gravelly voice which spoke brilliantly and, at moments, pedagogically; not a tall man, but with bulk that was hard, strong, and unyielding; he possessed a security within and a mastery of Marxist ideology. His intellect is broadly acknowledged; his warmth and charm recognized by those who knew him. Although Tina had been working more concretely in the militant revolutionary movement since Weston's departure, she now aligned herself with the Anti-Imperialist League of the Americas. She had participated in the "Hands-off Nicaragua" campaign established in Mexico City, and helped to found the first anti-Fascist Italian committee there. That same year she had become a member of the Communist party. Tina's emotional involvement with Vittorio Vidali was not to take place for several years. In part, a passionate devotion to the Communist cause and to the anti-Fascist movement motivated their friendship. Vidali also brought to their relationship an intellectual and spiritual strength which served Tina's needs at that time.

Her letters to Weston continued, although her communication with him was on a different level. In July 1927 she reported on a visit to a school; her observations, in view of the political difficulties of the time, are worth noting:

Some people—friends of Ella [Wolfe] here from New York—they wanted to visit the school in *Colonia de la Bolsa*. Since I was also anxious to know it I offered to take them—Edward when we left the place we all had tears in our eyes—What that Sr. Oropeza (the founder and director) has accomplished is something I will not attempt here to relate—And when we complimented him on his achievement he answered, "I could have done nothing without the children!" They have departments of Carpentering—Baking—Sewing—Printing—Photography—Farming—Shoemaking, etc. Everything on the smallest scale is certain but *serious*—each department has an expert person as a teacher—I mean a regular professional baker, shoemaker, etc. Everything is run on the basis of syndicates—every department has its delegate—they hold weekly meetings and discuss the problems arising during the week and the way to improve everything. They have a department of justice also elected by the boys and formed by the boys—One case is this: a boy was found stealing a considerable amount of money from the general funds—how do you suppose they punished the boy? By making him their treasurer—

Besides manual labor they all have certain hours for general instruction—and some for gymnasium, games, etc. I would write on and on about this but I would after all not be able to at all—Sr. Oropeza is writing a book on the founding and developing of the school—John Dewey (one of his greatest admirers) promised to finance the publication—

I am indeed sorry that we never visited the school while you were here as we had so often planned—

Dear one—this is all for tonight—

Tina still enjoyed communicating her news and thoughts about Mexico and their mutual friends to Weston. She continued her travels and her photography and was devoting more of her time to serious pursuits and not living the life of an expatriate. Given the reputation which Tina gained as a promiscuous, tempting woman, her behavior seems extraordinarily different from some American expatriates whose lives in other parts of the world were devoted to creativeness of a sort, wastefulness and phoniness in their defiance of the bourgeois world. But Tina's life was inner-directed; she was neither indiscreet nor indiscriminate, and she was possessed of a discipline, a drive and a capacity to respond to the life around her. She was also involved with a man who shared these qualities.

Tina's photograph reveals so much of Xavier Guerrero and at the same time so much of herself. Dominant in the beautifully carved face is the sense of mystery, of power, of all of Mexico's pride, of *Indianismo* which seems to be impenetrable. There is also the sensual fulfillment nourished and shared perhaps by Tina herself (p. 105).

Yet what dominated each of them at this time seems to have been their consciousness of a human struggle that was greater than their own private involvement. Xavier was later to leave

Mexico for the Soviet Union, where he remained for some years in the Lenin school in Moscow. We do not know whether it was Tina's intention to join him there, but they remained in close touch through letters, and Tina kept him apprised of events in Mexico by her own reporting and through periodicals she sent him. She was going through another momentous change in her life; she was living alone and eagerly embracing the new paths her life was taking, broadening the scope of her work in photography and political involvements. She had time as well for old and new friends. The renowned Mexican photographer Manuel Alvarez Bravo tells us what he found in Tina:

I met her for the first time in 1927. I was in Oaxaca where I worked during the years 1925–26. While in Oaxaca I received many magazines and other publications from Mexico City, and through them I learned about Tina Modotti, particularly through two magazines—one published by Gabriel Figueroa and Gabriel Fernandez Ledesma, who was also her friend, and Frances Toor's magazine, *Mexican Folkways*. I had been working in photography since 1924 and was very eager to meet her. In 1927 she had that same elegance and grace she had brought with her to Mexico. The walls of her studio were white and clean; later she started to write some of Lenin's and Marx's phrases on them. Even before that time on a visit to Mexico City I had seen an exhibition of Weston's photographs and of course there were also some of Tina's—this was during 1924 or 1925—they were in the romantic period (she had two periods—the romantic and the revolutionary).

One day a friend pointed out two people, Tina and Weston; each was carrying a camera. That was the first time I saw her, near *La Santisima* Church. They looked at the church but didn't take any pictures. That was my first glimpse of Tina, but I really met her in 1927 . . . I visited her on many occasions and she was generally very busy—meetings with people like Carleton Beals and Frances Toor but they were speaking English and I don't know how to speak English. But very often on a visit she would show me what she had done and what Weston was sending her and we would talk for a long while . . . At the meetings she conducted herself very gracefully and in fund-raising she would speak in Spanish and in Italian.

Tina was not only sympathetic to Manuel as an individual but was equally impressed with his work and unselfishly encouraged the development of his art. She sent some of his prints to Weston without identifying them. Weston responded with a letter addressed to M. Alvarez Bravo, asking pardon since he was not sure whether he was addressing a *Señor*, *Señora* or *Señorita*. He asked whether they had been sent for an exhibition in Germany for which he had been making a collection, or for his inspection. And his letter continued:

But no matter why I have them, I must tell you how much I am enjoying them. Sincerely, they are important —and if you are a new worker, photography is fortunate in having someone with your viewpoint. It is not often I am stimulated to enthusiasm over a group of photographs . . . I will not write more, until I hear from you—some explanation and word about yourself.

Weston added this comment in his Daybook:

> I have been the recipient of a package of photographs. Photographs of better than usual technique, and of excellent viewpoint . . . so many were of subject matter I might have chosen—rocks, *juguetes*, a skull, construction. I wonder if this person . . . does not know my work, or Tina's? In fact I had a suspicion—and still wonder—if these prints are not from Tina—under an assumed name—perhaps to get my unbiased opinion . . . it is all a very nice mystery.[2]

Tina's own work was being published; commendations and commissions were coming from all sides. She was happily earning a livelihood through photography and expressed her feeling about her work to Weston: "You don't know how often the thought comes to me of all I owe to you for having been *the one important being*, at a certain time of my life, and when I did not know which way to turn, the one and only vital guidance and influence that initiated me in this work that is not only a means of livelihood but a work that I have come to love with real passion and that offers such possibilities of expression (even though lately I am not making full use of these possibilities)."

At this time Tina was occupied with assignments from *Mexican Folkways* and with photographing the frescoes of Rivera, Guerrero, Máximo Pacheco and José Clemente Orozco. Orozco, who was then in New York, commissioned Tina to photograph particular sections of his frescoes, directing her as to the position of the camera in relation to his work. He communicated these instructions to Jean Charlot, and Tina would try to fulfill his wishes. "Tina's paraphernalia was old-

Yolanda Modotti, Tina's sister; San Francisco, by Tina Modotti. c. 1925

Vittorio Vidali (Carlos Contreras), USSR, by Tina Modotti. 1930–31

Diego Rivera addressing a meeting of the International Red Aid, Mexico, by Tina Modotti. c. 1928

Wine glasses, by Tina Modotti. 1925

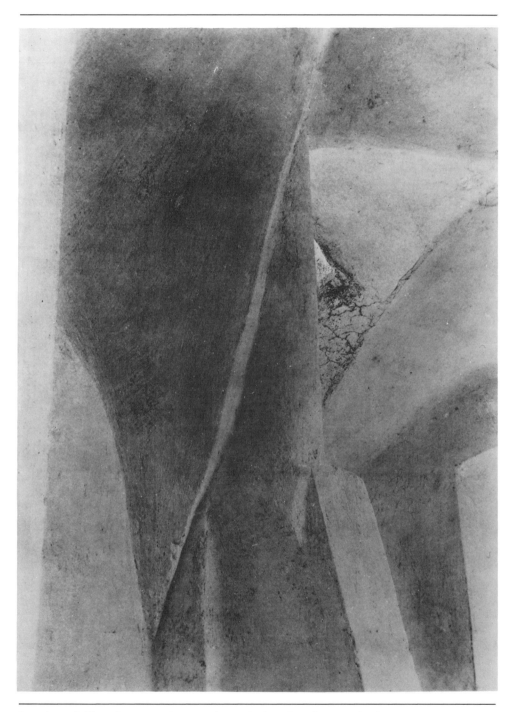

Interior of Church tower, Tepotzotlan, Mexico, by Tina Modotti. 1924

"Germination," detail of mural by Diego Rivera in Chapingo Agricultural School, Mexico. 1925

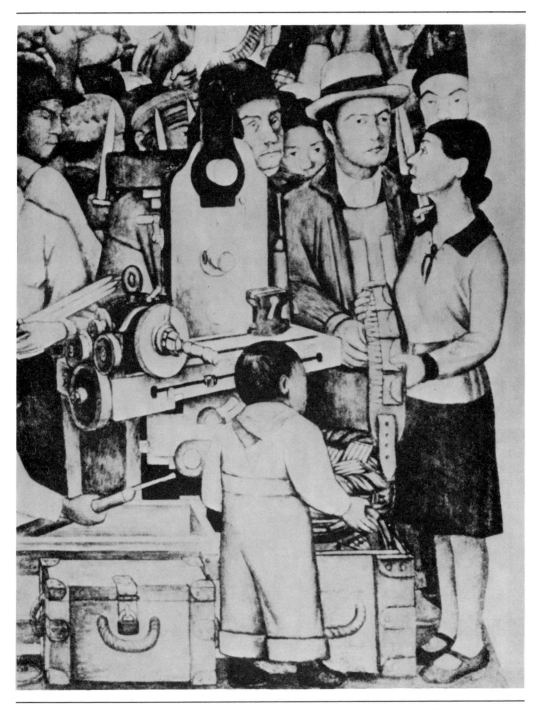

Detail of mural by Diego Rivera in the National Palace, Mexico, showing Tina distributing arms to the people

Head of Christ, Mexico, by Tina Modotti

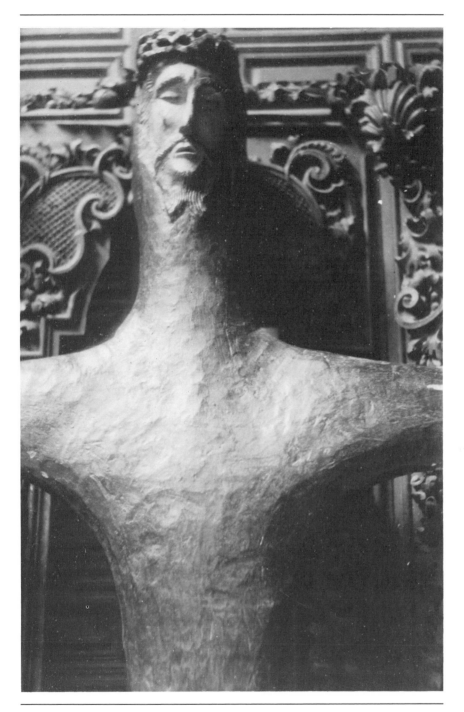

Crucifix in the Museum, Morelia, Michoacán, Mexico, by Tina Modotti. 1925

Hands of Marionette Player, Mexico, by Tina Modotti. 1926

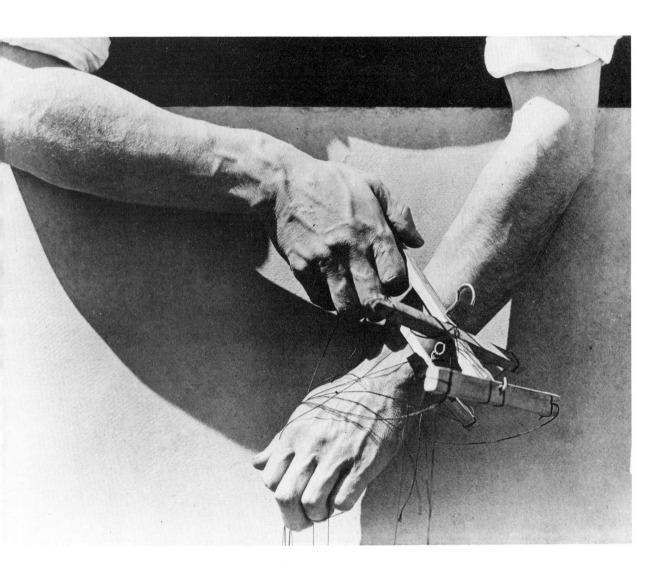

Hands of Marionette Player, Mexico, by Tina Modotti. 1926

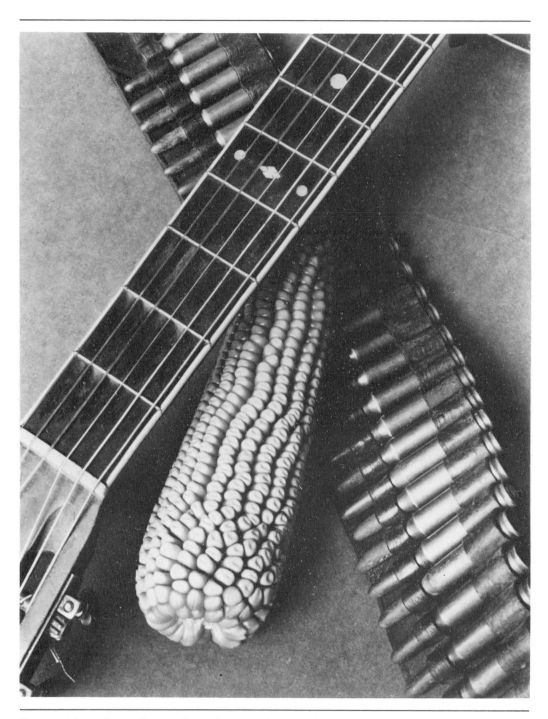

Composition: Corn, Guitar, Cartridge; Mexico, by Tina Modotti. 1928

fashioned even for that day, and it took much ingenuity to fit her bulky box camera and tripod along the staircases and under the low arches of the Colonial building."[3]

We know little of Tina's emotional and sexual involvements after Guerrero had left for the Soviet Union. We know from details revealed later that she had indeed professed her love for Guerrero. A woman like Tina, aware of her own sexuality, might indeed have enjoyed other encounters outside of the conventionalities of her time; going her own way, and obeying the passions within her.

Often she would work with the chief editor of *El Machete*, Rosendo Gómez Lorenzo. This newspaper had become the official periodical of the Mexican Communist Party. Tina volunteered to translate from Italian to Spanish, working directly with Gómez Lorenzo. He tells of an evening in the newspaper office when Tina was translating an article, with him typing and correcting as he went. Julio Antonio Mella entered the office and a formal introduction was made. Tina had met Mella before at a demonstration on the occasion of the execution of Sacco and Vanzetti and had known of Mella's political activity in his native Cuba. Gómez Lorenzo was aware of the mutual attraction of the two and invited Mella to join them for a coffee after their work was finished. They then accompanied Tina to her home at 31 Calle Abraham Gonzalez where she had been living alone. This was in June 1928; by the end of September of that year Mella was living with Tina.

Julio Antonio Mella, a young Cuban revolutionary, had been active since his student days in Havana against the dictatorial government of General Gerardo Machado (1925–1933). He had fled Cuba alone (his wife refusing to join him) and had sought refuge in Mexico. He was a student of law at the Universidad Nacional in Mexico and worked as a journalist.

In Mexico he found new emotions, and in Tina he found the woman to encourage and accompany a man of action. Their love flowered from the time and the place and was nurtured by the fine comradeship of belonging together to the Communist Party. They were individuals too and each constituted for the other a pledge for the future. After Weston, it seems as though Tina could only love a man who was fighting to change the world.

A battle fought with the heart is the most searing, and in making the choice of Mella over Guerrero, Tina found more than a comrade, more than a fellow artist. Guerrero was an inscrutable, impassive man; his solid frame and copper-hued skin belonged not to a man of action but to that strange brooding intensity of the Mexican Indian. He was a silent man; his gestures had an eloquence beyond words. If the basis of her personal commitments had become primarily political, given her own inner drives and sexuality and Mella's own obvious vitality, then the eventual transference of her affections from Guerrero to Mella is understandable. Mella, a young hero-figure among the left in his own country and in Mexico, had been forced into exile to pursue his dedication to a political cause. This guiding philosophy, together with the undeniable sexual attraction, might have provided complete fulfillment for Tina at this time of her life. She was alone, in the full bloom of her beauty, and by this time probably more easily accepting the changing realities of her life than she had been previously. It was not the adventure of loving that Tina pursued, it was love itself.

On the evening of January 10, 1929, anxious to see an issue of *El Machete* which contained an important article by him, Mella arrived at Rosendo Gómez Lorenzo's office and carried off the first copy. He mentioned to the editor that he had a rendezvous at a bar with José Magriña, another Cuban, who said he had some information about a possible attempt on Mella's life. Gomez Lorenzo warned him to be careful, saying that it might be something else. (Magriña later denied that this conversation had taken place.) Mella kept the appointment and later went to meet Tina at the cable office, reporting to her that the information he had received was vague and of no importance. Upon leaving the cable office, shortly after 11 p.m., Mella and Tina walked toward their apartment which was close by. Two shots were fired at Mella, the bullets penetrating the stomach and the thorax and left shoulder. Bleeding profusely, Mella staggered a few steps and then fell, breaking his left arm. He did not die instantly. An ambulance brought him to the Hospital San Jerónimo; an operation was performed in an attempt to save his life, but at 2.15 a.m. he died. He had said in those few moments of consciousness on the pavement, with Tina hovering over him, that it was Magriña and his political enemies who were the assassins. The rendezvous at "La India" was a setup to enable the assassins to follow Mella's movements.

In the following days, the right-wing press relentlessly pursued the case, exploiting it in the most sensational fashion. It is revealing to see how one such paper, *Excelsior*, today more liberal, used its columns without fear of libel or without any consciousness of journalistic ethics. The editor reiterated the paper's unbiased reporting and immediately announced that

Tina's version of the assassination contradicted the police version. The first morning headlines began:

FIRST REPORT OF MELLA SHOOTING

The Cuban Journalist Antonio Mella Gravely Wounded Last Night

Sr. Mella was hit by two bullets, one in the abdomen, double, penetrating the stomach and thorax, and the other in the left shoulder. In addition he suffered a broken arm when he hit the pavement after being wounded by the well-aimed bullets. According to information from friends of the victim immediately after the shooting, we learned that Julio Antonio Mella spent last night working in his office at 89 Isabel la Católica until just after eight o'clock when he suddenly told Sra. Modotti that he was in a hurry to meet Sr. José Magriña. Sr. Mella, accompanied by Sra. Modotti, went to see Sr. Magriña with whom he discussed several pending matters. After leaving Sr. Magriña, Mella took care of a few other errands, arriving near his home at about 10 o'clock ... There, suddenly he was attacked by two individuals who shot him, leaving him in agony on the sidewalk.

The next day's headline screamed that the assassination of Mella had produced a sensation in the capital and went on to add:

WHAT THE CUBAN STUDENT SAID BEFORE DYING

What Sra. Modotti says

Speaking at the sixth precinct, Sra. Modotti first gave another name, an American one, and then, afterwards, her own. In her first deposition she maintained that the

130

two individuals had fired from a passing car. Then she said that they had been on foot and had shot from behind, close enough for her to smell the gunpowder; nevertheless she has given no description of the criminals. Sra. Modotti's insistence on not naming the assassins gives rise to suspicions that she either knows the murderer of her lover, or knows who it was who ordered his murder. It is also said that there was one killer, and not two, as can be seen from the bullet holes, which are one above the other; had there been accomplices, the holes would be in different directions . . .

TINA HAS TRUE KEY TO CRIME was the accusatory headline in the Monday edition of the paper:

. . . according to police investigations, she is the one to have supplied the motive for the case, making it seem to have been a political crime. According to police officials, if the motive of the murder was not "passion," Tina Modotti must in any case know its cause and origin; if it was political, it is believed that the Italian (T.M.) must have been an instrument of enemies of the Cuban Communist.

Mella's lover is an extremely intelligent person; she is a woman who seems to be made of steel wrapped in skin: she is impenetrable, hermetic, closed to everything she doesn't want—or which is inconvenient for her—to say. If Tina Modotti insists on not telling the truth, we doubt any human effort will succeed in getting her to change her story, with her intelligence and with the ingenuousness with which she knows how to use her black eyes and flutter her lashes.

It is not hard to imagine how this kind of reporting affected Tina. The police had raided her apartment, and had confiscated letters and photographs; she was virtually under house arrest, guarded by two security agents. This reference to her use of "female wiles" at a moment when she was decimated by grief and was being daily subjected to vile accusations in court and in the press, must have been still another blow to her dignity and added to her contempt for the reporters.

In the same edition of *Excelsior*, there appeared a telegram sent by Portes Gil, then President of Mexico, who had been outside of Mexico City on the night of the murder, to the Secretary of the Communist Party of Mexico, assuring him of a complete investigation of the assassination. The next day, the 15th, *Excelsior* printed a scurrilous editorial:

ASPECTS OF A SENSATIONAL CRIME

The murder of the Communist student, Julio Antonio Mella, has caused great excitement in this city, in the whole country, and in Cuba. Until the present time, however, the criminal remains unknown because the only person who could identify him or give circumstantial evidence—the dead man's lover—remains suspiciously silent, declaring that she "did not see" the assailant, although the victim was shot at close range.

The crime would have been an ordinary one and would have attracted the public's attention only briefly, were it not for the fact that the Cuban government has been accused of the serious charge of homicide and complicity in the crime because Mella was an enemy of General Machado. Even the Cuban ambassador, Mr. Mascaro, has been hurt by the accusations, although those who

made them are a group of people without any represen-
tation amongst us, and who are notorious for the passion
and virulence of their openly demagogic and anti-social
tendencies.

Our government has shown impartiality and judicious-
ness; it has pledged protection to the Cuban embassy in
the event of possible attacks by Communists—who
pretend to glorify Julio Antonio Mella as the martyr of a
redeeming idea. It has also ordered the police to actively
carry out its investigations of the case so that it may be
solved and the criminal may not remain unpunished.

We do not prejudge, nor do we hypothesize; it is up to
the police and the courts to clarify the circumstances of
the crime. Meanwhile, we shall observe the prudent and
impartial attitude that behooves an honorable newspaper.
We shall, nevertheless, continue to inform our readers, as
we have in the past, of the progress of the case and of its
final outcome. The Cuban government maintains the
most sincere and cordial diplomatic relations with our
government. Both Cubans and Mexicans have common
origins; both deserve our deepest respect. It would not
be right that just because of the prejudiced and one-sided
declaration of those opposed to General Machado and
because Mella was his enemy, we should side with those
who, without any proof, disturb the authorities of that
country by accusing them of such a heinous crime.

In contrast to that attitude, those who in Mexico
boast of being Communists; those who have their eyes
fixed on Russia, as if it were the cradle and source of a
new civilization; those who without patriotism or national

solidarity are ready to submit themselves to the government of an alien regime and to accept the protection of any demagogue as long as he consorts with the Jewery of Russian Bolshevism; those Mexicans who ally themselves with nomadic foreigners, took advantage of the situation to declare emphatically, but gratuitously, that Mella was a victim of the Cuban government, a victim sacrificed on the altar of an ideal, deserving, thus, of consecration in the eyes of the world and of history.

In accordance with such a declaration, Communist groups (of both sexes, because women also participated) have assumed a hostile and injurious attitude against the Cuban government and its ambassador in Mexico. They add insult to injury by bringing up the well-worn theme of Yankee imperialism, and affirm that Mexico's press has sold out to the gold of Wall Street. As the Communists accuse General Machado and his representative amongst us of the latter charge, it must be emphasized that the indictment is ridiculous and absurd.

We have seen two extremely revealing photographs picked up by the police. One of Julio Antonio Mella and the other of his lover, Tina Modotti. Both photographs show these individuals completely naked, in an indecent pose that would be acceptable in shameless criminals and underworld figures, but not in an "apostle" of Communism, a redeemer of the people, or in his protecting nymph, Egeria—the guide and inspiration of the noble revolutionary.

And this fact—just this one—would suffice for upright and decent people to deprive Mella of posthumous honors and to relegate his mistress to the category of females who sell their love.

Is it not a folly to take Mella's side against the Cuban government when there is no basis to accuse the latter of the former's death? Where do the Communists' demonstrations and public injury come from? Have our police authorities perhaps given proof of partiality?

Let us await the judgment of the law and let us not anticipate reprehensible outbursts. Maybe this was a crime of passion and not a political one. If that were the case, isn't all this high-sounding oratory ridiculous; aren't the diatribes against the Cuban authorities unjust; and aren't the demonstrations of our "reds" and "red-blacks" unjust?

And the gold of Wall Street? Where is that famous gold, coveted by shabby individuals who feign to disdain it because they don't have any? The gold of Wall Street that corrupts the Mexican press! It must be like the sincerity of our Communists and the untarnished virtue of Tina Modotti.

In the same edition, *Excelsior* in its efforts to be "impartial," interviewed thirty people, none of whom believed it was a crime of passion. " 'The serious part is that while they're trying to build up a case for the idea of a crime of passion, they're losing time in the investigation. And it is quite possible that with this method,' the painter Diego Rivera told us, 'the remaining traces will be lost and the murderer will escape.'" At another point in the interview, Rivera said, " 'I also warned Mella to watch out, since he had received word that he was being followed by assassins. I even asked him to do me the favor of staying in at night. I thought it would be good to take precautions, and that he should always be accompanied by two young men from the Party, just in case. But since he was careless and brave, he paid no attention.'"

In discussing the Colt 45 pistol which was believed to be the murder weapon, and which had been said to have been in the possession of Tina Modotti, the American journalist Carleton Beals gave the newspaper a detailed account.

About four months ago, Mr. Lee Simonson Jr., editor of the New York art magazine *Creative Art*, wrote to me asking for material on the Mexican art scene, because he wanted to devote a special issue to the art of this country. Among other things, he wanted me to write an article on the photography of Tina Modotti and to send him all her best photographs so that he could reproduce them. I sent him the article, which as a matter of fact will be appearing in the next issue of the magazine. As soon as I received Mr. Simonson's letter I went to Tina's house to gather information and photographs. While I was getting the former, Fritz Bach, a German journalist, came by, and in the course of talking about various subjects not worth mentioning, Tina picked up a pistol that was on the work table and placed it in Bach's hands. He examined it, and I could tell he was interested in buying it. Mr. Bach tried to take it apart, but he couldn't. He asked Tina how the weapon worked and she told him she didn't know. Then Bach turned to me and asked me to show him, but since I don't know anything about guns I couldn't help him out.

Excelsior also interviewed Gloria and Max Campbell, who lived in the same house as Modotti. They heard Mella's cries, as did another woman, who operates a bakery close by on the same street. She thought the shots she had heard were tire blow-outs. On opening her window, she saw a boy running, and she heard Mella say that Machado and the Cuban Embassy were responsible for his death. She ran to the phone and called the Green Cross.

Excelsior continued:

"In the final analysis," according to one source, "Mella would have said nothing once he was mortally wounded, because he wouldn't have wanted to compromise Tina." According to sources who know Sra. Modotti through having cultivated her friendship, said lady is not of an age capable of exciting violent passions. She has been accustomed from an early age to earning her own living and to living independently—due to the fact that she was raised and educated in the United States; and, rather than unchecked love, she has brought respect and intellectual devotion to those she calls her "companions."

Among the latter, we heard the names—Mella was the last—of men who were by no means uncultivated but, on the contrary, had a total awareness of life. For them, Modotti has not been the physical woman, but the special, preferred friend who understood and stimulated them. Her socialist ideas—we were told—are sufficient explanation for her alliance with Mella. "Tina," said one of the group we interviewed, "never allowed herself to be dominated by a man in the ordinary sense of the

word; yes, for a man with a mind she would have affection,
a meeting of spirits; but nothing more.''

Sr. Gómez Lorenzo had denied in an interview that Mella ever received money from Magriña. He asserted that Mella answered Magriña's call because he wanted to find out how things were going in Cuba.

Sr. Lorenzo had warned Mella to be very careful with Magriña, because Magriña came from a suspicious political background and it wouldn't be at all surprising if he were a spy for the Cuban government.

The article continued:

Regarding the conduct—way of life—of Julio Antonio Mella, his friends told us yesterday that he was so involved in political propaganda work, projects he was either creating or directing—constantly giving conferences, attending meetings, editing correspondence—that they don't understand how he found time for all his activities.

To summarize: the friends and co-workers of Mella maintain that it is not a case of a crime of passion and that even though the investigation being conducted by Mexican authorities is pursuing this course, they should not abandon the idea that it was a political crime.

On January 16, accompanied by Diego Rivera as well as by the security agent who was vigilant in his "guarding" of her, Tina arrived in court for an official interrogation which was carried verbatim by the paper:

Q. On what date did you first meet Julio Antonio Mella?

A. I can't tell you exactly, but it was during the Sacco and Vanzetti campaign, at the beginning of last year, in this city. Not that at the time we were close; I had been introduced to him and we would say hello to each other, that's all.

Q. *On what date did he first ask you to make love with him?*

A. Last year, in June; I agreed last September.

Q. *Were you involved with anyone else at the time?*

A. I was not spiritually tied to any other person when I liked and loved Mella. Before that I had ended a previous commitment.

Q. *Do you know Xavier Guerrero?*

A. Yes, I met him in Los Angeles, California, where he had been asked by the Secretary of Industry to mount an exhibition of popular art in 1923.

Q. *What were his political ideas?*

A. He was and is a Communist, affiliated with the Mexican Communist party.

Q. *Who do you think had stronger ideas about Communism, Mella or Guerrero?*

A. Both.

Q. *Are you sure?*

A. Absolutely.

Q. *Don't you consider it a violation of a person or of a love to write love letters to someone else? In other words, being in an intimate relationship with one person, don't you abuse him in writing of love to someone else?*

A. Yes.

Q. *Did you love Guerrero very much?*

A. In his time, yes.

Q. *Can you tell us whether Guerrero was very much in*

love with you?

A. Yes, I can. But the love he had for me was less than the love he had for the fundamental love of his life, the revolution. He was ready to die for it.

Q. *Do you believe that when someone feels love for someone, he is willing to sacrifice her for another?*

A. If the person is worthy, yes. The love of revolutionaries is not separate from their other activities; it is related to their political ideals.

Q. *When you began to have intimate relations with Mella, did you break off completely with Guerrero?*

A. Yes. That is to say, I kept sending him weekly newspapers for his activities.

Q. *And you didn't send him any letters?*

A. Absolutely not. Only periodicals. I wanted him to be up to date on politics in general in Mexico.

Q. *What was the form of the break-up between yourself and Guerrero?*

A. A definitive letter.

Q. *Did you ever tell Mella about your relationship with Guerrero?*

A. Yes, right at the beginning, because I was going through a tremendous conflict. Mella didn't understand the struggles I had to go through to reach a point where I could decide to be his companion. Those months of hesitation were incomprehensible to him, and he interpreted them differently. It's not exactly that I was hesitating because I still loved Guerrero. . . . In fact, after Xavier had been gone a week, I thought about it at length and I freely resolved to stay with Mella.

The judge, Attorney Pino Cámara, wound up the examination of the witness with the following question:

Q. *When Guerrero left, did you have any other suitors?*

A. No, none.

The deposition finished, Tina Modotti was escorted back to her house by the agent. *Excelsior* continued its coverage with the following:

Wasn't it a crime of passion? It is possible, since, of those under suspicion by the police, one is the dead man himself, who with his double personality (Julio Antonio Mella used this name in Mexico—his name in Cuba was N. McPartland) facilitated the betrayal; and the other, Senor X, is still in Moscow and is the painter Xavier Guerrero, the first lover of Tina Modotti. Whether it be political or whether it had a different motive, the Mella murder will only be understood if the Venetian Tina Modotti decides to break the impenetrable silence, the firm hermeticism within which she has locked herself, and reveals the identity of the mysterious person who accompanied them down Avenida Morelos, along the Paseo de la Reforma, and into Abraham Gonzalez, where he fired the two shots that killed her friend.

The newspaper had in some way obtained copies of two letters: one in which Mella spoke of his intense love for Tina, the other a carbon of a letter from Tina, the original of which was sent to Senor X, Xavier Guerrero (to whom that pseudonym belongs)*, telling him she no longer loved him because she loved another.

The newspaper quoted these letters because they considered

---

*This salutation was of course not a pseudonym but merely the abbreviation of Xavier.

them the basis of the investigation of Tina. The letter signed by N. McPartland (Mella) and sent by him from Oaxaca said in part:

Sept. 11, 9 p.m.

My dear Tinisima, Just a few lines after the telegram . . . You may feel it was careless of me to send the telegram, since you're accustomed to being terrified by what there is between us, as if it were the worst crime in the world. Nevertheless . . . nothing more right and more natural . . . and . . . more necessary for our life. Besides, I thought it important for you to receive these lines the very same night. No?

I haven't forgotten your face once on this whole long journey. I still see you "in mourning"—clothing and spirit—saying your last goodbye as if you wanted to come toward me . . . .

And then appeared the text of the letter to Xavier Guerrero (written shortly after her decision to be with Mella) which also was ready into the testimony:

Mexico, September 15, 1928

There is no doubt that this will be the most difficult, most painful, and most terrible letter I have ever written in my whole life. I've waited a long time before writing it, mainly because I wanted to be very sure of the things I am going to tell you and secondly, because I know from the start the terrible effect that this will have on you.

I need all the calm and serenity of spirit I have to explain to you clearly, without ambiguities; and above all, to keep myself from getting emotional, which would be inevitable if I let myself think of what this letter represents for you.

X., sometimes when I think of the pain I am about to cause you, I feel more like a monster than a human being; and I'm sure you will think this is true. At other times I see myself as the poor victim of a terrible fate, with a hidden force that acts on me, despite myself, the way it acts on life. But I would be the first to reject these elements: "fate," or "hidden force," etc. Well then, what remains? What is it that I am? Why do I act in this way? I sincerely believe that I have intrinsically good feelings, and that I've always tried to do good for others before I've thought of myself, not to be cruel for its own sake. That's the proof that when I have to be the way I'm being with you now, I suffer (perhaps more than you) because of the consequences.

But I should tell you what it is I have to tell you: I love another man. I love him and he loves me, and this love has made it possible for something to happen which I thought could never happen: to stop loving you.

X., I could tell you at length the whole history of this love, how it began, how it evolved, how it reached the point where I resolved to tell you about it; how I have even fought with myself to extirpate it from my life (I swear to you, even to the point of considering suicide if it could have provided a solution that would not have been cowardly). I could tell you, in short, all the tortures caused by this terrible dilemma I have had to face. I've thought of everything, and principally of you (this won't offend you, I'm sure). I've thought even more of the effect this step will have on revolutionary action. This has been my greatest worry, greater even than my worry about you. Well, I've come to the conclusion that however it turns out, whether I'm with you or with someone else, here or in some other place, whatever small use I can be to the cause—to our cause—it will not suffer, because the work for the cause is not the reflection or the result of loving a revolutionary, but a deep-seated conviction within me. For which I owe you a lot, X. You were the one who opened my eyes, you were the one who helped me when I could feel the pillar of my old beliefs shaking beneath my feet. And to think that for all the help you gave me, this is how I pay you. How terrible!

X., the only thing that gives me any comfort is knowing that you are very strong and that you will be able to overcome the pain I cause you. I ask myself now whether you will doubt the sincerity of how I loved you. X., I swear to you on the sacred life of my mother that I loved you as I have never loved before in my life, and I swear to you that my feeling for you was the greatest pride of my life. And yet despite this, what has happened has happened. How was it possible? I myself do not know, I do not understand it, but I do feel that what is happening now is a clear and inevitable reality, and that I can do no less than what I am doing. I thought of waiting to tell you this verbally on your return, here; or else to go to where you are to tell you. I thought that that would be more honest and more loyal than to tell it to you through this letter. But I realized that to go on writing to you in the tone that was always so natural, but which would be pretending, would mean to deceive you, and I respect you too much for that. And also I cannot, should not, deceive you nor betray the present reality. . . .

What is the nature of the woman who has written this letter —a poignant, self-searing portrayal of her true self? No heroics here, but a courage born of honesty and bearing the burden of a love gone; the self-reproach accepted, with an acknowledgment of a specific guilt rather than any singular acceptance of guilt; a woman who had known love and friendship; who knew the elusiveness of love and treasured the depths of friendship.

Letters of protest to the editorial were sent to *Excelsior* by trade unions, women's groups and individuals, among whom were Miguel Covarrubias and Diego Rivera. They demanded an interview with the Director of the paper, and the following day the headline stated:

THE PHOTOGRAPHS OF TINA MODOTTI AND JULIO A. MELLA, ACCORDING TO VARIOUS ARTISTS

They are Not Immoral Pornographic Nudes But Artistic Nudes, According to Authors of Declaration

(As a sign of our sincere impartiality we have made room for the following declaration, leaving full responsibility for its ethical content up to its authors)

—We refer to your editorial of yesterday, January 15th:

Certain photographs of nudes which were found in Tina Modotti's house led your reporter to describe both Sra. Modotti and Julio Antonio Mella with epithets

which are an insult to the dead man and to a woman who has no way of defending herself.

In addition—and this is the point which prompted our action—this attack sets a dangerous precedent against free professional expression for artists in all forms: in sculpture, in painting, in dance, in theater. It is impossible to maintain that the nude in and of itself is immoral; if that were true, fifty percent of the world's greatest works of art would have to be condemned.

To defend our rights as artists, we approached the most distinguished professionals in Mexico and showed them the Modotti photographs which might have been those referred to in your editorial. We obtained, in writing, the opinion of all these respected artists whose reputation is well established both artistically and morally; all of them were in favor of artistic nudes and against the opinion expressed in your editorial.

These written opinions were brought last night to the offices of Excelsior, *after we had asked that they be published in the name of impartiality; but we were told that this was impossible since the edition was already closed. Today, the 16th, at noon, we returned to* Excelsior *with the written opinions and the proofs of all the nude photographs taken by Tina Modotti, which we did not believe to be the ones upon which your columnist had based his conclusions. We asked to see the ones he had used, but Senor Espinosa said he did not think he could comply with our request. He arranged an appointment for us at 6 o'clock with Senor Rodrigo de Llano, director of* Excelsior, *to discuss the matter. We were warmly received by Sr. De Llano, who was kind enough to show us the photographs in question. One of them shows Julio Antonio Mella naked in front of a shower door, and was taken to fulfill the entrance requirements of a Rowing Club in Havana. Julio Antonio Mella, who was one of the best rowers in that city, must have had the picture taken just as atheletes all over the world have their pictures taken in sports clubs all over the world. This photograph was taken over three years ago, before he had even heard of Tina Modotti, who obviously had nothing to do with it. As far as the other photograph is concerned, it is an artistic nude, the work of a photographer Edward Weston, who is recognized as the greatest artist in his field in America today. Sra. Modotti posed for the photograph, working as a professional model for her teacher, Weston.*

We asked Sr. De Llano why the documents of an investigation—which is the only way these photographs could have been requisitioned by the police—happened to be in the editorial offices of Excelsior *and not in court or in the offices of the police, Sr. De Llano replied that* Excelsior *had received these photographs anonymously. The fact that, as Sr. De Llano told us, the photographs were conveyed anonymously to* Excelsior, *shows exactly the intentions of whoever sent them; the fact that they were not taken by either Tina Modotti or Julio Antonio Mella converts the assertions and interpretations contained in yesterday's editorial into absolute lies with no value whatsoever.*

The director of Excelsior, *with whom we discussed*

*all these points in our meeting with him, has kindly
offered to publish this declaration. We hope it will be
inserted in a position equivalent to that occupied by the
editorial to which we have repeatedly referred. In advance,
our deep thanks to Sr. Rodrigo de Llano.*
Mexico, D.F. January 16, 1929
Miguel Covarrubias
Diego Rivera

Excelsior also printed their interview with Magriña:

*"But we have also been told that when Mella fell
down wounded he said that you knew everything . . ."*

"Nobody has heard that he says that."

"Tina Modotti assures it."

*"Don't you think they've been irresponsible not to
have followed out the possibility that Tina Modotti is a
Fascist spy, and that Xavier Guerrero, the man of the
letters, is in Moscow? Couldn't there have been a plan
on the part of Mella's own friends? They say Modotti
has been a Fascist spy . . ."*

And turning to certain details of the slaying, to the exact
moment when it was carried out, *Excelsior*'s reporter asked
Magriña to give his opinion on the veracity of Tina's statement
that it was impossible for her to see the assailant. Magriña
declared Tina to be lying, adding that in his opinion, "When
a person is attacked from behind, the first thing he or she does
is to turn around to see who it is. At least that's what I would do,
even if I was arm in arm with my father and I had to attend
to him after seeing that he had just been wounded."

The reporter explained to Magriña that one of the most
serious charges against him was that it appeared very plausible

that he could have followed Mella home after their meeting, or that he was already waiting for them at the site where Mella was shot.

"Have you seen," we asked him, *"Diego Rivera's accusations against you which appeared in one of the morning papers?"*

"This man Rivera doesn't even know what I look like, to go around making accusations like that. All the accusations that have been made against me are of that type. I can't give them any importance. When I come before a judge, then they'll see all their lies destroyed, one by one."

Pepe Magriña had been apprehended and imprisoned briefly as the agent-provocateur behind the assassination. The police had found the newspaper *El Machete* on Mella's body, as well as a paper bearing Magriña's address and telephone number, but he denied that he had sought the rendezvous and that it was indeed Mella who approached him regarding the newspaper *Cuba Libre*. He was later released.

For Tina, the damage had been done. Her name had finally been cleared. The complicity of the Machado government, together with the apparent complicity of the Mexican police, was recognized, and it brought about the dismissal of the Chief of Police in charge of the investigation. Relations with Cuba were ruptured by the withdrawal of the Cuban ambassador. But the blatant accusations of the editorial, compounded by the indignities of the cross-examinations hurled at her at the hearings, started a vendetta of slander in the rightist press that continued and indeed was to reappear at the time of Tina's death twelve years later. She must have written the details of this period to Weston: his entry for the day February 21 in his

Daybook states that he has received "a letter from Tina disclosing her strength through a terrible ordeal: she has maintained and proved her innocence."

After only four months of a fulfilling and rewarding relationship, Tina was left alone again to face not only the loss of a love but the vilification of her whole life. Yet when she wrote in March to Weston, her first thoughts were about Brett, who had broken his leg in an accident. "Monna just told me of the terrible news about Brett. I am so upset that I cannot think clearly—is he better? Will his leg be normal again? Poor boy, I cannot quite grasp this misfortune—it seems so terrible! Please give him my deepest sympathy and tell him I feel for him with all my heart! And for you, Edward, too! I know how much you must feel and suffer! I have gone through so much suffering myself lately and my heart is so full of pain and bleeding that it makes me all the more receptive to the suffering of the beings which are dear to me."

The letter continued:

> Oh Edward, for a few moments to be near you—to be able to give vent to all the pent-up emotions which gnaw at my heart—you might not agree with all I would say—that does not matter—but you would understand the tragedy of my soul and feel with me—and that, not everybody can do!
>
> But I cannot afford the luxury of even my sorrows today—I well know this is no time for tears; the most is expected from us and we must not slacken—not stop halfway—the rest is impossible—neither our consciences nor the memory of the dead victims would allow us that—I am living in a different world, Edward—

strange how this very city and country can seem so utterly different to me than it seemed years ago! At times I wonder if I have really changed so much myself or if it is just a kind of superstructure laid over me. Of course I have changed my convictions, of that there is no doubt in the least, but in regards to mode of living, tastes, new habits, etc.—are they just a result of living in a certain environment, or have they really taken the place of the old life? I did not make this very clear; I mean: are these new habits taken up in order to keep pace with the new environment, or have they really taken the place of the old life? I have never stopped to question this before and I cannot understand why I am doing it now; I guess dear it was just a desire to talk with you a while like in the old times . . . P.S. There is something I have been forgetting to tell you in my last letters—Things are very insecure here for "pernicious foreigners." I am prepared for the worst—any day they may apply the "33"* on us—I want to have all my things in shape as much as possible. What shall I do with all your negatives?

What is underneath this questioning of herself? There does not appear to be regret for either the demands or the consequences of the political life she has chosen. Perhaps this is a moment when she is overcome by the events of the last year and, as was her custom, her letters to Weston become a sounding board for the questioning and clarification of her own thinking.

Tina was continuing to make her livelihood through photography. Her photographic eye was much in demand. She had

---

*Article 33 of the Mexican Constitution, adopted in 1917. "It defined foreigners and their rights, stated that they could be expelled from the country by the president if their presence was considered 'undesirable' and listed certain transactions in which they were forbidden to engage." (E. V. Niemeyer, Jr. *Revolution at Querétaro*, 1974, University of Texas Press, p. 196).

the priceless ability to intuit and communicate. At the same time she was able to record the essence of a time and place with clarity and discernment. In a sense hers was an original eye, seeing Mexico not from the viewpoint of an outsider, but with a compassion and personal knowledge and involvement. Her work had been used in the magazine *Mexican Folkways* since 1927, and even outside of Mexico her work was much sought after. She received invitations from the *British Journal of Photography* and Pacific International Salon of Photographic Art. *The Revue Mensuelle Illustré* "Varietés" in Brussels published her work as did the art magazine *Creative Art*, in New York, with an article by Carleton Beals which appeared in February 1929. Requests for her photographs came from Prague as well, and the Agfa Paper Company sought her endorsement of their photographic paper (August 1929).

In September of 1929 she reported to Weston:

> I am still in Mexico but it is so disagreeable not to know how much longer one is allowed to remain, it makes it almost impossible to make plans for work, but of course the wisest attitude is to simply go on, do everything one intends to do as if nothing was ever going to happen to spoil one's plans . . . I am thinking strongly to give an exhibit here in the near future; I feel that if I leave the country, I almost owe it to the country to show, not so much what I have done here, but especially what *can be done* without resorting to colonial churches and *charros* and *chinas poblanas*, and similar trash most photographers have indulged in. Don't you think so, dear? By the way, had I ever told you that I was offered the position of official photo-

Mother and child, Mexico, by Tina Modotti. 1926

Indian mother and child, Mexico, by Tina Modotti. 1926

Mother and child, Oaxaca, by Tina Modotti. c.1929

Baby nursing, by Tina Modotti. c.1929

Muchacho with sombrero, by Tina Modotti. c.1927

Baby, by Tina Modotti. c.1926

Girl carrying pail, by Tina Modotti. c.1926

Two children, Mexico, by Tina Modotti. 1927

grapher of the National Museum some months back? Well, tempting as the offer was, I could not accept it. Many have criticized me for the refusal, but both as a member of the party and as companion to Mella, it would have been impossible. The government here did absolutely nothing to bring about justice when they had all the opportunity in the world; they had the most responsible guilty one in their hands and they let him go free. Anyway, as far as work is concerned, I have always plenty of it, in fact more than I can do, considering that I cannot give all my time to photography.

Obviously, Tina's strength and personal convictions allowed for no compromise. On November 5th in a letter signed by the artists Carlos Orozco and Carlos Mérida on behalf of the *Dirección de Acción Cívica* of the Federal District of Mexico, Tina was formally invited to present her work, and she accepted the opportunity. The exhibition was inaugurated by the Rector of the *Universidad Nacional Autónoma de México* in the National Library, and Tina's work was lauded in many publications; several photographs were reproduced and she was hailed as an original force in photography. One of the most important comments came from Gustavo Ortiz Hernán, then a young critic, now Director of *El Universal Gráfico*. He stated:

Without a doubt the photographs of Tina Modotti are highly personal and distinct. Ideologically she belongs to the avant garde and the extreme tendencies of the social movement of which she is counted among the most significant followers. Her integrity and her courage were demonstrated on the occasion of the assassination of Julio Antonio Mella. Her photographs can be easily classified: works of pure composition in which concerns for perspective, construction and dimension reveal the skill of the artist in handling her medium. Composition of flowers, of jars, of tools form a special kind of still life handled with great plasticity. There are two special photographs which should be given the title of "Revolution"—a perfect synthesis of a great social ideology: an ear of corn, the neck of a guitar, and a cartridge belt [p. 126] are juxtaposed in one; in the other, a sickle takes the place of the guitar —the photographic qualities undiminished by the substitution.

In another category is a particularly magnificent photograph—a group of crystal wine glasses is composed [p. 118], their photogenic qualities combined with a rhythm and musicality which is attained by an association of ideas. The power of suggestion is enormous in this photograph—the perfect synchronization of transparencies is magnificent.

In another group, the scenes of our daily lives— construction sites, stairs, stadium, wires—which we look at indifferently—acquire an almost exotic prestige and a unique personality. The photographs of Tina Modotti are symbolic of the eagerness and anxiety of the new young to know everything, to examine everything and to revise it.

On the occasion of the exhibition and publication of her own work, Tina had said, "I consider myself a photographer, nothing more ... Photography, precisely because it can only be produced in the present and because it is based on what exists objectively before the camera, takes its place as the most satisfactory medium of registering life in all its aspects, and from this comes its documental value. If to this is added sensibility and understanding and, above all, a clear orientation as to the place it should have in the field of historical development, I believe that the result is something worthy of a place in social production, to which we should all contribute." This viewpoint is particularly important when we learn later of her reactions to street life in Berlin and her stated inability to function as a reporter. She was dedicated to an expression in which aesthetic and political sensibilities were united.

Tina's exhibition attracted accolades not only from her fellow artists, but also from the thousands of workers who passed in awe before her irrefutable denunciations of the living conditions of the poor. David Alfaro Siqueiros, before the end of the exhibition, gave a lecture on December 14, 1929, under the title, "The First Revolutionary Photographic Exhibition in Mexico." Describing the strength and beauty of Tina's work, he spoke of the true meaning of photography in Mexico—"the art form which mirrored and retained what it saw and offered through the purity of her expression the surprise of being able to look at what the viewer had previously only seen." Tina reported to Weston, "I wish you had heard S's conference. It was great. Such profound knowledge of the history of art through the ages and such a vital and significant viewpoint. We were surely smart in getting the program presented. But after the government, the University and all the Mexican politicos pride themselves on their 'revolucionarismo,' they couldn't very well refuse."

Of great interest to the artists and intellectuals, not only in Mexico but throughout Europe and the United States, came the news of Diego Rivera's expulsion from the Communist Party in the autumn of 1929. There had never been a logical, official, or even a personally coherent account from Diego himself as to the causes of the break. Even as late as 1961, Bertram Wolfe indicates in his *The Fabulous Life of Diego Rivera* that "the causes were international in origin. Diego was caught in a world-wide purge emanating from factional politics in the Soviet Union, involving in some countries the exclusion of whole parties, in others expulsion or resignation of the principal leaders and founders. . . ." He goes on to add that Diego was also accused by his fellow party members of "working on the public buildings of a bourgeois government, and of accepting from its hands the post of director of the School of Plastic Art." This expulsion was the kind of news which Tina would most naturally report to Weston, as well as reporting Diego's marriage to "a lovely nineteen-year-old girl of German father and Mexican mother, a painter herself" (Frida Kahlo):

> But the most startling news about D. is another one which will be spread through all the corners of the world tomorrow. No doubt you will know of it before this letter reaches you. Diego is out of the party. Only last night the decision was taken. Reasons? That his many jobs he has lately accepted from the government, decorating the National Palace of Fine Arts, are incompatible with a militant member of the party. Still the party did not ask him to leave his posts, all they asked him was to make a public statement that the

Mella's typewriter, by Tina Modotti. 1929

Men reading *El Machete*, signed by Tina Modotti. 1929

Meeting of the "Hands-off Nicaragua
Committee," Mexico, by Tina Modotti. 1926

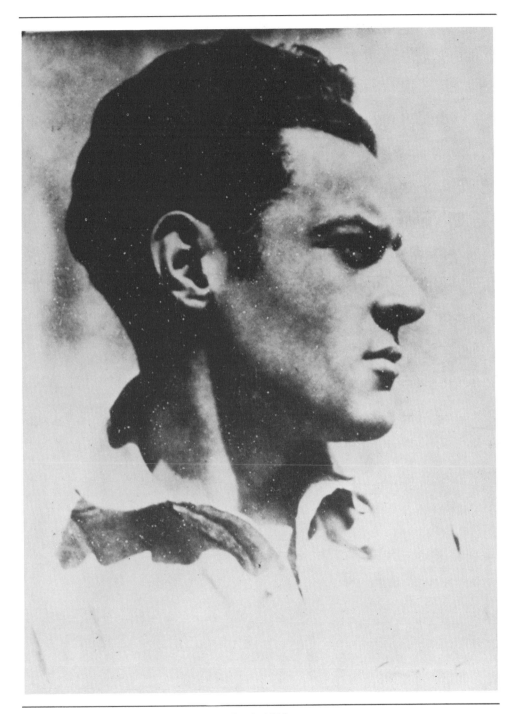

Portrait of Mella, signed by Tina Modotti. 1928

holding of these jobs did not prevent him from fighting the present reactionary government. His whole attitude lately has been a very passive one in regard to the party, and he would not sign the statement so out he went. There was no alternative.

There are so many sides to this question. We all know that he is a much greater painter than he is a militant member of the party, so the party did not ask him to give up painting, all they asked him was to make that statement and live up to it. We all know that all these positions were thrust upon him by the government precisely to bribe him and to be able to say: "The reds say we are reactionaries, but look, we are letting Diego Rivera paint all the hammer and sickles he wants on public buildings." Do you see the ambiguity of his position? I think his going out of the party will do more harm to him than to the party. He will be considered a traitor. I need not add that I shall look upon him as one too and from now on all my contact with him will be limited to our photographic transactions. Therefore, I will appreciate it if you approach him directly concerning his work. Hasta luego, dear.

The importance of this letter lies not only in the information about Diego, who had been considered the "Lenin of Mexico," but in the completeness with which it reveals Tina's strict adherence to Communist Party decisions.

It has been obvious from the tone of the editorial in *Excelsior* on the occasion of Mella's assassination that the political situation in Mexico had regressed and the gains of the last several years were being seriously eroded. The Soviet Union had been accorded recognition in 1924, but the attitude toward the Mexican Communists and political refugees from other countries had been getting progressively less sympathetic. Red-baiting, so blatant in the editorial in *Excelsior* in January, 1929, had been spurred by the breaking of diplomatic relations between the Soviet Union and Portes Gil's government in that year. The Communist Party was declared illegal; some of its leaders were slain, others jailed. Mexico was anxious to rid itself of the "fierce and bloody Tina Modotti," and in February of that year a situation arose which provided the opportunity.

On Sunday, February 5th, Pascual Ortiz Rubio was inaugurated as President of Mexico. After the inauguration, he left the *Palacio Nacional* to ride in the Bosque de Chapultepec with his family. Six shots were fired at him; they missed. "Although the youth (Daniel Flores—23 years old) who had fired the shots was apprehended, all attempts were made to relate this crime to the work of more intellectual people."

Tina was accused of being part of a conspiracy in the attempt to kill the President and was arrested. As a condition to remaining in Mexico, she was asked to abandon her revolutionary ideas. Imprisoned for thirteen days, she went on a three-day hunger strike in protest. At the end of this period she was "administratively" expelled from the country and sentenced to deportation. She was given just two days to straighten out her affairs and even during that short period her house was being watched by the police. The numerous protests of workers, peasants and intellectuals did not help her cause. But Tina was without a usable passport. Officially, American citizenship was available to her through her marriage to Robo, but she was not in possession of an American passport. Upon request for a

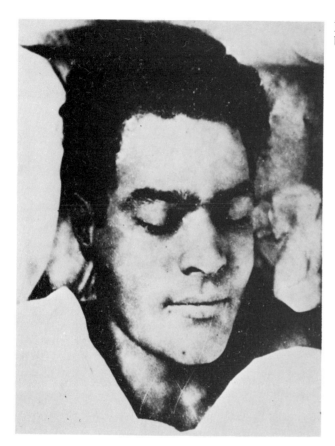

Death portrait of Julio Antonio Mella,
by Tina Modotti. 1929

Tina accompanied by Diego Rivera on
way to police hearings, Mexico. 1929

visa to the United States, the U.S. ambassador, Dwight W. Morrow, offered one under the condition that she abandon her political activities. She rejected the proposition. At the Italian embassy she was also offered a new passport with the following notation—"valid only for a return trip to Italy"—sure death for an outspoken anti-Fascist. Finally, she was able to leave for Europe on a weather-beaten Dutch ship, the "Edam." Before she was to leave by train for the port of Vera Cruz, Manuel Alvarez Bravo, her long-time friend, was with her.

I learned that she was leaving and went to see her; I was the only person who was with her in her house. There were police; I don't remember well, but there were a lot of police—about four or five to take her to the station. She was still very agitated and very nervous. She was finishing putting her things in order so she could leave. Then, since she was throwing a few things out . . . well, with embarrassment I asked her if I could keep a few of the things she was throwing away (some of her photographs). She said yes; she told me smiling—she still smiled even though she was very nervous. She was always very polite and very friendly. Since I couldn't go with her in the same car in which the police and she were going, I went to the station. I got there first, and it gave her great pleasure to see me. I hadn't told her that we would see each other again in the station. She took a window seat and I sat down next to her in the train, and when the whistles blew I got off and waved to her from below. She was still very nervous but still in those moments of farewell she showed the same friendliness and warmth as always.

Couple at zoo, Berlin, by Tina Modotti. 1930

1930-1939
Germany, the Soviet Union, Spain

4 It was no ordinary passenger ship on which she sailed; the "Edam" sailed from Vera Cruz with Tina on board as a detainee. She wrote to Weston on February 25th:

I suppose by now you know all that has happened to me, that I have been in jail 13 days and then expelled. And now I am on my way to Europe and to a new life, at least a different life from Mexico. No doubt you also know the pretext used by the government in order to arrest me. Nothing less than "my participation in the last attempt to kill the newly elected President." I am sure that no matter how hard you try, you will not be able to picture me as a "terrorist," as "the chief of a secret society of bomb throwers," and what not . . . But if I put myself in the position of the government I realize how clever they have been; they knew that had they tried to expel me at any other time, the protests would have been very strong, so they waited for the moment when, psychologically speaking, the public opinion was so upset with the shooting that they were ready to believe anything they read or were told. According to the vile yellow press, all kinds of proofs, documents, arms and what not, were found in my house; in other words, everything was ready to shoot Ortiz Rubio and unfortunately I did not calculate very well and the other guy got ahead of me. This is the story which the Mexican public has swallowed with their morning coffee, so can you blame their sighs of relief in knowing that the fierce and bloody Tina Modotti has at last left forever the Mexican shores?

Dear Edward, in all these tribulations of this last month, I often thought of that phrase of Nietzsche which you quoted to me once. "What doesn't kill me, strengthens me," and that is how I feel about myself these days. Only thanks to an enormous amount of will power have I kept from going crazy at times, as for instance when they moved me around from one jail to another and when they made me enter a jail for the first time and I heard the slamming of the iron door and lock behind me and found myself in a small iron cell with a little barred skylight, too high to look out from. An iron cot without a mattress, an ill-smelling toilet in the corner of the cell and I in the middle of the cell wondering if it was a bad dream . . . They gave me only two days after the 13 in jail to get my things ready;

you can imagine how I left everything, fortunately my friends all helped me so much; I can't tell you how wonderful they have all been to me.

I am still in a kind of haze and a veil of irreality permeates over everything for me; I suppose in a few days I will be normal again but the shocks have been too brutal and sudden.

Two weeks later she was to write again, from the U.S. Immigration Station in New Orleans:

I cannot even remember when I wrote you last, so much has happened in these past weeks and such unexpected things too—as for instance my presence here—but I have gotten to the point where I just accept philosophically what comes along. You know the old saying: "It never rains unless it pours"; well that just about fits my condition at present. I thought that after 13 days in jail in Mexico City—followed by two days (all I was granted to get my things ready), and after being taken to Vera Cruz and put on a boat, via Europe, my troubles would be over—but no indeed—in the first place I learned that the boat employed one month and a half for a voyage that could be done in three weeks —but since on this boat, passengers are accidental and its specialty is cargo, we stop at all the following ports: Veracruz, Tampico, New Orleans, Havana, Vigo, Coruña, Boulogne Sur Mer, and at last Rotterdam. This would not be so bad if I traveled as a normal passenger, but in my condition of being expelled by the Mexican government I am strictly watched in all ports and not allowed to touch shore, excluding this port where the U.S. Immigration authorities brought me here, and here I am relegated for eight days, that is till the damned boat gets through its loading and unloading.

It was not just will power that Tina had; she also possessed that rare ability to stand aside and look with wry humor at her situation, commenting:

> I hope, Edward, that you enjoyed a good laugh when you heard I was accused of participating in the attempt to shoot Ortiz Rubio—"who would have thought it, eh? Such a gentle looking girl and who made such nice photographs of flowers and babies . . ." I can just imagine the comments of this order being made by the readers of Mexico's yellow press on reading all the sensational "information" headed by huge titles on the front pages, calling me "the inquiet Communist agitator," "the celebrated photographer and Communist," and so forth—*El Universal* of Mexico City, among other things, published the following: " . . . in the home of Tina Modotti, the authorities found documents and plans which clearly indicate that her intention was to commit a crime similar to Daniel Flores on the person of our President, Ing. P. Ortiz Rubio; and her not having carried out her intention is only due to the fact that Daniel Flores got ahead of her . . . " (Can you beat that?)
>
> The truth of the whole matter is this: The Mexican government was eager to expel me but they need a good pretext, so they took advantage of the attempt to shoot

Ortiz Rubio and profited from that psychological sentimental-hysterical state which public opinion is full of during any public commotion—I am wondering dear if I have already written you all this—perhaps so—as I said before, I have forgotten when I wrote you last. The place I am in now is a strange mixture between a jail and a hospital. A huge room with many empty beds in disorder which gives me the strange feeling that corpses have laid on them—heavy barred windows and door constantly locked this last one—

The worst of this forced idleness is not to know what to do with one's time—I read—I write—I smoke—I look out of the window into a very proper and immaculate American lawn with a high pole in the center of it from which top the Stars & Stripes wave with the wind —a sight which should—were I not such a hopeless rebel—remind me constantly of the empire of "law and order" and other inspiring thoughts of that kind—

The newspapers have followed me, and at times preceded me, with wolf-like greediness—here in the U.S. everything is seen from the "beauty" angle—a daily here spoke of my trip and referred to me as "a woman of striking beauty"—other reporters to whom I refused an interview tried to convince me by saying they would just speak of "how pretty I was"—To which I answered that I could not possibly see what "prettiness" had to do with the revolutionary movement nor with the expulsion of Communists—evidently women here are measured by a motion picture standard—Well my dear, I must stop now—the bell is ringing for supper

—and the matron (who suffers from diabetes, poor soul) will come for me any minute to escort me to the dining room where she doesn't take her eyes off me for fear this "terrible radical" might escape her and infest the country with poisonous propaganda. . . .

She concludes her letter with her assurances that she will forward an address in Europe—as soon as she has one—and adds her customary devotion to Weston sending as well a big hug to Brett.

"I am on my way to Europe and to a new life, at least a different life from Mexico," she had written. This unemotional reporting of her detention and expulsion, the matter-of-fact tone of her assurance of survival, is extraordinary in the face of the anguish Tina must have felt after being wrenched from what had been her home.

There is no erosion of will in this woman, in spite of her uncertainty about the future. She had been cut off from the three countries that had nurtured her—Italy, her homeland, to which she longed to return, the United States, and Mexico. She was no longer an individual who was an artist. She had become a political person. She was thirty-four years old, alone, seeking asylum, faced with still another crisis point in her life. What was the reality which gave her the strength to face the future? She had been strongly individualistic from childhood, never shirking the responsibilities which had been thrust upon her—indeed perhaps seeking out responsibilities had been a part of her character from the beginning. But she was essentially a private and not a public person. The tragedy of Mella and the exposure in the press and subsequent deportation had changed all that, but had not affected her perseverance.

When Tina finally arrived in Holland after a voyage of four weeks, the authorities there did not allow her to disembark. The Italian Embassy, acting on the authority of Mussolini's government, demanded that she be extradited immediately to Italy. The workers' organizations in Holland put the matter into the hands of a strong group of lawyers and at the same time demanded asylum for Tina. At last she was permitted to go ashore with orders to leave Dutch territory the same day.

Her comrades in the Communist party arranged for her to be admitted to Germany and she arrived in Berlin on April 14, 1930—to a Berlin that was quite different from that William Shirer had once described:

> From 1927 onward there was a general prosperity in Germany. A wonderful ferment was working there. Life seemed more free, more modern, more exciting than in any place I had ever seen. Nowhere else did the arts or the intellectual life seem so alive. In contemporary writing, painting, architecture, in music and drama, there were new currents and fine talents. And everywhere there was an accent on youth. One sat up with the young people all night in the sidewalk cafes, the plush bars, the summer camps. . . . The old oppressive Prussian spirit seemed to be dead and buried. Most Germans one met—politicians, writers, editors, artists, professors, students, businessmen and labor leaders—struck you as being democratic, liberal, even pacifist.[1]

This was a Germany which Tina might have found conducive to making a new life for herself, but by 1930 all had changed. The Wall Street crash in the United States in 1929 had drastically weakened the German economy. By 1930 unemployment was on the rise and taxation was strangling the people, especially the common working man, on whom the food tax placed the heaviest burden. The depression gave the Hitler movement its great opportunity, even though by 1930 the Communists in the elections had over four million votes and seventy-seven seats in the Reichstag.

Mr. and Mrs. Witte were among the first people Tina contacted in Berlin. We do not know who they were, but we know from Weston's Daybooks that they had visited Mexico in the mid-twenties and had purchased several of Weston's and Tina's photographs. Apparently Tina had remained in touch with them through the years, and they had always reminded her that they had a room all ready and waiting for her. "How can I praise sufficiently that exquisite and heavenly creature called Lady Witte? She emanates such a spiritual beauty that the best of one is stimulated by her presence," she had written. But Tina felt that she could not burden her friends and found a room, very convenient and private, where she hoped to live cheaply. She had no idea about remaining in Germany; she knew she had to make a living and she also wanted to be where she could be most useful to the movement. She wrote of her dilemma to Weston. "The idea of portraiture in Berlin rather frightens me; there are so many really excellent photographers here, and such an abundance of them, both professional and amateur, and even the average work is excellent; I mean even the work one sees in the windows along the street . . . I have been wondering if I could not work out a scheme by which to get a sort of income from the blessed U.S. Perhaps by contributing to periodicals, magazines, etc. I feel that if Frau Goldschmidt gets around one hundred marks for articles in the New York Times, I should be able to do the same."

Her reaction to the situation in Berlin was one of admiration for the Teutonic stubbornness and self-sacrifice in the face of economic stress. She noted that the people never laughed, but walked the streets very gravely, always in a hurry, and seemed to be conscious of a heavy burden. Berlin had indeed changed from the 1927 described by Shirer.

The city itself she found very beautiful, even though "I have not seen the sun once during my ten days here and for one coming from Mexico the change is rather cruel. But I know that the wisest thing is just to forget sun, blue skies and other delights of Mexico and adapt myself to this new reality, and start, once more, life all over . . . "

She asked Weston if he knew some photographers in Berlin, and wryly commented, "I well know of course that it is not good policy to look up photographers if one is also a photographer, but all I would want from them is practical advice as to purchasing materials and find a place to do some printing, etc. If possible I never again want to go to the trouble of fixing up a dark room, and I hope to be able to work in some dark room. If I was in the U.S. I would become a member of the photographers' association and make use of their work rooms; perhaps something like that exists here. I shall see." In a postscript she added, "I must beg you to divulge as little as possible my presence here. It might cause me trouble in the future. Thanks!"

One wonders, however, if she did not know the great photographers who, from all points in Europe, were assembled at the Bauhaus during this period. The Bauhaus was the first great institute for design. By 1930 it had been in existence ten years and was racked, from inside and out, by political tensions. Although the director Hannes Meyer had dissolved the Communist cell of students within the Bauhaus in March of that year, he himself was removed because of his supposed Communist activities (in his open letter to the Lord Mayor Hesse of Dessau Meyer stated the futility of his assurances that he had never been a member of any political party). Tina did not indicate that she met Hannes Meyer at that time, although we know that she did meet him later in the Soviet Union. Their friendship was renewed in Mexico and endured until she died.

The work in photography produced by the Bauhaus masters would certainly have surprised Tina for the innovative ideas expressed, and for their attitude toward the camera as an instrument in the service of a world where man had to make peace with the machine. Artists such as Moholy-Nagy, from Hungary, experimenting in photograms; Piet Zwart, from Holland, working with collage; Herbert Bayer, from Austria; Alexander Rodchenko, from the Soviet Union; were among the most avant garde painters-designers-photographers. Their work went beyond that of documentary reportage and propaganda. Weston's work had been exhibited along with Moholy-Nagy's in New York. Weston had extremely negative reactions to Moholy's experiments, and perhaps this kept Tina from contacting him and the Bauhaus group.

On the other hand, Weston and Tina were pioneers in Mexico. They had introduced photography as an art to a fresh and appreciative audience. In Germany and all through Europe photography had been acknowledged as art, widely practiced and widely appreciated for several decades. The Vienna Salon of Photography was held in 1891 (the work of Alfred Stieglitz was prominent in this exhibition). In Paris the First Exhibition of Photographic Art was held in 1893. The Zurich Dada group had produced photographic abstractions without a camera since 1918 and both Man Ray, an American working in Paris, and Moholy-Nagy, in Germany, were making rayograms by 1921. André Kertesz, a Hungarian living in Paris, was focusing his camera on unposed people and their surroundings, shooting, as he saw it, the fleeting instant. In Germany photomontage was an important device of John Heartfield, who applied it first to surrealism and later to political ends.

Perhaps all this had an intimidating effect on Tina and her photographic eye during the period of change and stress. By the fourteenth of May she joined the Unionfoto G.m.b.H., a professional photographers' association, and was issued a press card. But her photographic troubles were many, as she described in an undated letter.

> I have been offered to do 'reportage' or newspaper work, but I feel not fitted for such work. I still think it is a man's work in spite of the fact that many women here do it; perhaps they can, I am not aggressive enough. Even the type of propaganda pictures I began to do in Mexico is already being done here; there is an association of "workers-photographers" (here everybody uses a camera) and the workers themselves make those pictures and indeed have better opportunities than I could ever have, since it is their own life and problems they photograph. Of course, their results are far

from the standard I am struggling to keep up in photography, but the end is reached just the same.

I feel there must be something for me but I have not found it yet. And in the meantime the days go by and I spend sleepless nights wondering which way to turn and where to begin. I have begun to go out with the camera, but *nada*. Everybody here has been telling me the Graflex is too conspicuous and bulky; everybody here uses much more compact cameras . . . I have even tried a wonderful little camera, property of a friend, but I don't like to work with it as I do with the Graflex: one cannot see the picture in its finished size; . . . anyway buying a camera is out of the question . . . besides, a smaller camera would only be useful if I intended to work on the streets, and I am not so sure that I will. I know the material found on the streets is rich and wonderful, but my experience is that the way I am accustomed to work, slowly, planning my composition or expression right, the picture is gone. . . .

I was advised not to give an exhibition till fall, that being a better time; by then I would like to have something of Germany to include.

She also noted with surprise that most photographers still used glass plates. The different standards of measurement confused her—"a hell of a mixed-up affair," she declared. This technical difference compounded the difficulty of language barrier.

I tell you I have almost gone crazy. I had to buy an enlarger apparatus and enough "tools" to work with. I did this unwillingly since I wanted to feel that I could pick up and go whenever I felt like it (or whenever I was forced to . . .) now I feel in a way tied down to my dark room . . . I needed to find a furnished room since I absolutely refused to invest in furniture also, and with another room next to it, with *water*. I underlined the water part because one ought to be in Berlin to realize the difficulty of finding rooms with water. At last I have what I needed: of course the furnished room is not fit for a studio, but since I am going to try getting along without making portraits, I don't need a studio.

Her unspoken fears and insecurities were always there to contend with, and she cautioned Weston in replying, "please *do not* put my name on the outside envelope."

A few days later, on receipt of a letter from Weston, she addressed him as "Dear 'grandfather,'" congratulating him and declaring, "if you had the little imp near you you would just play with him, or her, with the same precious youthfulness which belongs to you." And on another subject she states:

Oh how happy I was to hear from you. A few days ago I wrote you again but now I almost regret having sent it; I was in such a despondent state of mind and weak enough to not just keep it to myself and made you the victim of my weakness. Please forgive me, and do not worry about me; I will fight my way and the last word has not been said yet, and all these trials will bear some fruit, I am sure; in other words I have enough self-confidence and realize I must not undervalue my capacities. Only there are moments, who doesn't have them? when everything appears black (perhaps they are black and those are the moments of lucidity) but

> maybe next day the sun shines and the little birds sing,
> and the panorama changes as if by magic!

These are words of a strong, courageous woman regretting her moment of self-pity for her solitude, and even able to add greetings to Sonia Noskowiak (then Weston's companion) and the boys.

Like all her letters to Weston since their physical separation, this one also contained "professional talk."

> I was interested in your decision about the glossy paper. Yes, I can just picture the "pictorialists" lifting their arms in horror at this new "outrage" by this terrible terrible iconoclast Edward Weston! So far I have undertimed everything I began to make; this damned light after Mexico! And yet I had accounted for it; but I will know better in the future!

Apparently Weston had written to her about his reprinting of old negatives on glossy paper. These exchanges are fascinating, since it is difficult from Weston's Daybooks to see how the practically unbroken exchange of correspondence reveals the essence of their enduring friendship.

Tina had considered the camera as "the most satisfactory medium of registering life in all its aspects." She had already expressed admiration for the workers-photographers in Berlin. Germany, particularly Berlin, must have seemed alien to her Mediterranean eye and heart. In the few photographs we know from the Berlin period, we note that she could not function merely as a reporter. Without the time necessary to study and describe the social conditions around her, street life in Berlin seems to have brought out a touch of ironic humor and detachment in her. This can be seen when she observes the man and woman at the zoo and the nuns in juxtaposition with the nude statue. (pp. 170, 186). There was little she could respond to, little to evoke a human emotion or create the remarkably romantic yet accurate reportage which was characteristic of her work. Only in the landscape (p. 192) perhaps is there a deep response to her new environment—to the verdant majesty and grand scale of forests so unlike the sculptured earth of Mexico.

Happily, at this time she began to meet some of the photographers and writers. When Lotte Jacobi, another fine photographer, showed Tina's photographs in a special viewing in her studio, one of the critics wrote:

> The secret of her work was that she made the world visible by her vision—this vision meant that the sad eyes of a poor child might be more beautiful than that of a ballet-queen; that industrial landscapes, the means of production, the fields of sugar cane, rice, jars, hands, guitars, hats . . . are more beautiful than the green avenues of Switzerland. Only the men of this world are not happy. Why? This is the question one senses in her photographs.

He was obviously moved by Tina's profound revelations of the Mexicans' particular sensibility. He must have responded to her power to evoke a sense of place, of time, to be able to absorb her subject as though she had contemplated it deep within her and then was able to give it form. It must have been evident to him that Tina was unafraid of registering the honest sentiment she felt.

Essentially, Tina must have felt an unease in that turbulent year in Berlin. Although many of the German people were

Street scene in Berlin, by Tina Modotti. 1930

bound by their loyalty to defend the democratic Republic, Hitler continued to gain political support. The September election returns showed support of over six million, which entitled the National Socialists to 107 seats in the Reichstag, thus making it the second largest in the parliament. The Communists had also gained, their representation in the Reichstag increasing from fifty-four to seventy-seven seats.

But clearly the Nazis had captured millions of followers and were making headway in the Army. The elections marked a turning point; Germany was on the road toward the Third Reich. It was impossible to ignore the Nazi movement and the obvious transformations within German society. The deteriorating economic conditions, and the accompanying insecurity— since she could not as a foreigner find regular employment which suited her abilities—must have motivated Tina to leave Germany after a six-month stay. Besides, she had few close friends there. Her friends in the Communist Party, particularly Vittorio Vidali, arranged for her to go to the Soviet Union, and she left Germany, arriving in Moscow in October, 1930.

Three months later (January 12, 1931), Weston received this communication:

I have been living in a regular whirlpool ever since I came here in October; so much so that I cannot even remember whether I have written to you or not since my arrival. But at any rate, today I received the announcement for your exhibit (just three months later due to the carelessness of the person who forwards my mail in Berlin) and I cannot wait one day longer to send you *saludos* with the same feeling of always! I have never had less time for myself than right now; this has its advantages—but also drawbacks, the main one being the utter lack of time to devote to you, for instance, if only through a few badly scribbled words. There would be so much to write about life here, but *no hay tiempo*—I am living a completely new life, so much so that I almost feel like a different person, but very interesting. Edward, as I wrote the above, I just got an idea, I swear it had never entered my mind before. Do you know of anybody that would buy my Graflex, very cheap? I could sell it here easily but the impossibility to get this size films makes it impossible. I need not add that it is as good as new and if you could find a buyer I would find the way to send it to you, people come and go daily. It has a Tessar lens 4/5 – 2 magazines, perhaps one can get one hundred dollars for it, and if necessary even less. I want to sell it so as to buy me a ''Leica.'' Forgive this interruption. What I meant to say still is that I like immensely the short introduction to the leaflet announcing your exhibit. So different and so intelligent! So at last New York enjoyed the treat of your work! [at the Alma Reed Gallery] I wonder if you plan to remain in Carmel indefinitely? Dear Edward, if ever you feel you are in the mood for a few words to me, the Berlin address is still good, only if possible, write compact, for many reasons—How are the *muchachos*? And Sonia? My best thoughts to you all—Tina.

Weston had indicated on the original of this letter—''Tina's last letter to me.''

The letter is remarkable for several reasons. She had stated, ''I am living a completely new life, so much so that I almost feel like a different person." Had this new life become so all-engrossing and had she become so different that she could cut off abruptly a channel of communication which had nurtured her for many years? Their correspondence must have been a lifeline for Tina, a bridge between her, her photography, and the world of thought she shared with Weston. Yet this was, according to Weston, the last letter he received from her. She had never, in any of her letters, sought to proselytize him with her political beliefs, although she had always made it quite clear to him where she stood. Had he in his ever-growing dislike for "the masses" become tired of this exchange? She remarks, "if ever you feel you are in the mood for a few words to me"—it is possible that his correspondence with her had lapsed. Tina was constantly on the move, but her family in California had heard from her, although unsteadily, until her death. Weston had known of her involvements with Guerrero and Mella, as she knew of his liaisons. Had her relationship with Vittorio Vidali meant so much to Tina that she could not continue her communications with Weston? She might have feared to involve Weston in a political situation; still, did she not feel in the rupture of her correspondence with him a more aching sense of loss than in their physical rupture? These are questions to which no one knows the answers, since no accounts exist to enlighten us. Accepting the fact that this was the last letter Weston received, it is almost impossible to believe that it was the last letter Tina wrote to him.

Also remarkable in the light of later events is her desire to buy a new camera so that she could go on with photography. And yet we know (at least we have no evidence to the contrary) that she abandoned her camera some time after 1931.

Ernestine Evans, at the time an editor with J. B. Lippincott in New York, had written in February of 1931 to Jacob Doletsky of Tass in Moscow, "I have asked Tina Modotti who is one of our best known American photographers to come and show you some of her Mexican photographs. I am certain that both you and Press Cliche will be interested in her work. I think she ought to be using her camera during her stay in Russia." Miss Evans had been the editor for *The Frescoes of Diego Rivera*, which was illustrated with Tina's photographs, and was familiar with all of her work. Many Americans, among them Fred Ellis, an artist, and his wife Ethel, visiting and working in the Soviet Union at that time, had occasion to meet Tina, who was presented to them as a photographer from Mexico. She was apparently close to the people in the film world in Moscow, so that her reputation and work were known and acknowledged.

Throughout the twenties there had been creative ferment in Moscow, and it must have been important to Tina to discover the social context in which this ferment was born. Her own political and creative growth had taken place in Mexico, where the arts flourished at the same time that social progress through upheavals was gained. And her participation in both had produced works of tremendous impact.

On the other hand, the camera as a recording instrument was a dynamic challenge for the artists in the Soviet Union and quite different from Tina's approach to the camera, although she had made what she called propaganda pictures. We know from the work of Alexander Rodchenko, who had been at the Bauhaus, that experimental photography played an important part in the developing arts in the Soviet Union as early as the early 1920's; photomontage was used in magazines, in posters for both film and political purposes. Its great strength as a modern revolutionary expression made it appropriate for use on the agit-trains as they sped through the remote parts of the Soviet Union in order to reach the illiterate people living outside the larger cities.

Perhaps Tina was unsure and modest about her own work. She felt that photography had to be tied to one's own roots. Confronted with the great revolutionary experiment unfolding before her eyes, she may have decided that she had to become a participant in that experiment through her own education and politically-oriented work before she could again use her camera.

She was not alone in Moscow. It was there that she resumed her friendship with Vittorio Vidali, whom she had originally met in Mexico in 1927. This friendship turned to love—a new love that was very closely identified with her own roots and her political passions for Italy and for the world. With Vidali's guidance, she became involved again with the Mezhrabpom, the International Red Aid in Moscow, as she had been in Mexico. The Communist Party also had offered her a very good job as a photographer but she refused it, choosing instead to devote herself to her own political education and to revolutionary activity.

Paul Strand, the great American photographer, has said that he always had an interest in the things that make a place what it is—not exactly like any other place and yet related to other places. Perhaps Tina too felt this and felt as well that a photographer's attitude toward life affects what her eye sees. Thus, perhaps it is not too difficult to understand Tina's

Landscape outside Berlin, by Tina Modotti. 1930

decision to abandon photography. In Mexico and in the Mexican revolution, Tina had been a part of the revolutionary struggles. Her camera was her tool; she understood its every nuance. She felt deeply the struggles of the people and she identified with those struggles. She was too briefly in Germany, and perhaps Germany was too alien to her, for her to be more than an onlooker. She had indicated that she could not truly function as a reporter—her camera could not reveal what her being could not absorb.

When Lotte Jacobi visited Moscow in 1932, she renewed her friendship with Tina. Finding her so completely occupied with political work, she asked how Tina, a fellow photographer with similar devotions to the art of the camera, could so completely abandon her work. Tina explained simply but firmly, "I cannot use the camera when there is so much work to be done." This reply surprised Lotte Jacobi at the time but in retrospect (1974) she understood it. It seems obvious from what we know of Tina that she felt she was born with an obligation to act—and that as a revolutionary, her commitment to the cause was her first obligation at this time. After all, she must have felt a great need to be part of that new reality which hopefully would point the way to reshape the world in her lifetime.

From that period onward, Tina worked for the Soviet International Red Aid—within the Soviet Union and wherever in Europe that organization could function. There is little doubt that not all of Tina's travels were in the service of the organization, but that she also functioned on special missions for the Comintern. In abandoning the camera she had abandoned a career of almost ten years, during which she rose from a pupil and apprentice to the status of a recognized artist.

When Jay Leyda, the eminent American film historian, was about to leave for the Soviet Union in 1933, Alma Reed asked him to take the monograph of Clemente Orozco published in 1932 with an introduction written by her. She also begged him to take a large package containing Tina Modotti's photographs which she had been holding for some time. Leyda was much impressed with Tina's work and looked forward to meeting her in Moscow. He of course contacted Sergei Eisenstein in Moscow, who was sure to know how to locate Tina. At that time Eisenstein was completely absorbed in his great movie *Que Viva Mexico* (*Thunder Over Mexico*), which he made in 1931. He explained to Leyda that while he knew and admired Tina he had seen relatively little of her, since he was protecting his Mexican film and did not want information about his friendship with Tina to filter back to Mexico or to his American critics. Both men studied the photographs Leyda had brought with him and both were impressed by her work. Leyda sought Tina out and found her living quite contentedly in a small room in a Moscow hotel which was reserved for party functionaries.

"She appeared vivacious and apparently suffered no loss of freedom in the tiny room she occupied," he states. How easy this is to understand! After the expulsion from Mexico, the brief though insecure stay in Berlin, Tina had indeed found not simply a refuge but a home, physical and spiritual. In her new relationship with Vidali and her acceptance in party work she had found a security and a direction which must have afforded her the profound sense of peace she had been lacking since her expulsion from Mexico. Leyda found that "there was no loss of political belief in Tina—she was almost monumental as a political worker as indeed she was monumental as an artist.''

He believes that the decision to abandon photography at that time was entirely hers—she felt that she could not be both a political worker and a photographer. She had made a decision and this in itself restored confidence and hope for the future, missing in her since the assassination of Mella.

By 1934 Tina left Moscow with the hope of settling in Spain and joining Vidali, who had been there since the proclamation of the Spanish Republic in 1931. Since the fall of the monarchy, Spain had seen riots in Andalusia, monarchist plots against the Republican government, the rise of the Falange, the separatist movement in Catalonia, along with those early reforms which the Republic had begun to achieve. A program of agrarian reform, which meant the expropriation of some of the immense holdings of the absentee nobility and the Church, had been started in spite of the difficulties. The feeding, clothing and education of the young in secular (rather than religious) schools and the right of women to vote, were among the early accomplishments.

Still, the young Republic could not change overnight a land which Pierre von Passen has described as "peopled with hundreds of thousands of monks, treasure-stuffed monasteries and churches, and overcrowded jails, a land filled with typhus and malaria; men and women dressed in rags. . . .'' Still the *Guardia Civil* shot down the strikers and were posted all along the roads and in the woods to prevent the hungry and poverty-stricken masses from attempting to occupy the seigneurial farms. Yet because the Communist Party of Spain, founded in 1921, was not yet a strong factor, it was not formally suppressed, and many Spanish Communists returned from exile. In spite of this, upon arrival in Spain Tina was apprehended by the *Guardia Civil* and taken back to the border.

Edouard Daladier, then Premier of France, had had a brief flirtation with the left wing of the Radical Socialists, and undoubtedly it was in this period that Tina was permitted to enter that country. Settling in Paris, she earned her living by translating and continued her work in the revolutionary movement through the International Red Aid organization. She helped to organize demonstrations and aid for the victims of the Floridsdorf uprising in Vienna, those who had been able to flee after the betrayal of the trade union strike in February 1934;* for the exiled Austrian miners and their families after the revolt in Spain in November of that year; as well as for those French revolutionaries who were working to establish a popular front in France. (The Comintern policy from 1934 onwards was to establish an alliance of all left-wing parties, the working class as well as the bourgeoisie, to resist Fascism. It was at the Seventh Congress of the Comintern in Moscow in July 1935 that the Popular Front was formally voted as a policy.) She told friends that since she had come a little late to the movement, she had to work more diligently, tirelessly, in helping the many political refugees of all nationalities who were gathering in Paris during that period.

In 1934 Tina helped to organize demonstrations in Paris for Thaelmann, a German; Dimitrov, a Bulgarian; Rokosci, a Hungarian; Gramsci, an Italian; Mooney, an American; Prestes, a Brazilian; Ghioldi, an Argentinian; and for countless lesser known political emigrés of all nationalities.

By the end of 1935 Tina was able to return to Spain to join

---

*"Here the insurrection ends, here, revolution begins." Stephen Spender, *Vienna*, Random House, New York, 1935, p. 25.

Vittorio Vidali and to enlist in the struggle against the continuing erosion of Republican Spain. The second uprising of the Austrian miners had, in October of the previous year, established the Union of Working-Class Brothers and succeeded in the creation of a revolutionary Soviet throughout their province. Their revolution was completely quelled, as were the uprisings in Madrid and Barcelona, and civil war was inevitable.

After the October 1934 insurrection, a Committee of United Action was formed with the primary objective of liberating, through amnesty, 30,000 political prisoners. It was followed by months of intensive work and polemical struggle and the government had to call for new elections. On January 15, 1935, the Communist and Socialist parties together with the young Socialist and Communist organizations, the General Workers Union (UGT) and other groups, had signed the pact that created the Popular Front, and thus brought about the unification of the working class.[2]

Hugh Thomas has written of this period:

Observe how in February 1936, the two sides which by then had taken shape in Spain and which referred to themselves by the military word 'front,' put their quarrels finally to the test of the polls, and . . . how the narrow victory of the Popular Front had brought in a weak but progressive Ministry, regarded by its own Socialist and Communist supporters as a curtain-raiser to far-reaching social and regional change. The elections of February 16, 1936 gave to the forces of the left 269 deputies out of a total of 473 in the new Cortes; a clear majority.

Here were ranged the masters of economic power in the country, led by the Army and supported by the Church, that embodiment of Spain's past glory. All these believed that they were about to be overwhelmed. Opposed to them were the "professors"—many of the enlightened middle class—and almost the entire labour force of the country, maddened by years of insult, misery and neglect, intoxicated by the knowledge of the better conditions enjoyed by their class comrades in France and Britain and by the actual mastery which they supposed that the working class had gained in Russia. Tragedy could not have been avoided.[3]

On July 17, 1936, Vidali was returning from a trip to Paris to consult with some leaders of the "Red Aid" there, and upon arrival at the airport in Madrid he was informed by several of his comrades there to meet him that the military rebellion had begun. The headquarters of the Madrid "Red Aid" (*Socorro Rojo*) were filled with comrades who had arrived there from all corners of Spain for a meeting to discuss organization. Vidali asked them to disband, return as soon as possible to their homes, and put themselves at the disposal of the Popular Front. Tina was already at work in the *Hospital Obrero* (Workers' Hospital), which had been abandoned by the Fascist doctors and religious nurses. Here she functioned as cook, director of personnel, and was ready to tend the wounded when they arrived. There in the kitchen of the hospital it was feared that the enemy might perpetrate a monstrous crime against the hundreds of wounded arriving from the Sierra. Simone Tery recalled how Tina said shortly before her death in Mexico, "I shall never forget the arrival of the first wounded *milicianos.* . . ." She said no more, but I saw the expression of anguish in her face as she evoked that first contact with war." Tery had originally met Tina in Moscow, where she was known to her only as Maria, and later in Spain and Mexico.

The famous Fifth Regiment was founded and commanded by Vittorio Vidali, known in Spain by his *nom de guerre,* Carlos Contreras. Tina enlisted in the Fifth Regiment, and worked with the International Brigade, made up of Communist and non-Communist volunteers, which had become the main work of the Comintern. She was active on the front, in cities and villages which had to be evacuated, on the roads organizing help for the soldiers and refugees. She also continued her work as a reporter—not as a photographer—for *Ayuda,* a weekly newspaper edited by the "Red Aid" of Spain, as well as for the Children's Home. She was known to all only as Maria. And she worked especially with the first Italian volunteers—refugees who formed themselves into the Gastone Sozzi Battalion—men and some women who were of no particular political grouping.

Later, the Garibaldi Battalion of the International Brigade, composed of all the left-wing parties, attacked the Italian Fascist infantry at Brihuega, outside the Madrid highway, but at first the Garibaldi men used this occasion to urge through loudspeakers and leaflets that *fratelli nostri* (our brothers) desert the Nationalist cause. If they came with their arms there would be an extra financial reward! It was the Italian prisoners who willingly talked about the extent of Italian intervention in the war.

Margarita Nelken, writer and deputy to the *Cortes* in Spain, later wrote:

For good, for absolute good, without restrictions or reservations, she was a revolutionary—a revolutionary in the most hidden fibers of her being . . . Tina Modotti, day by day during years and years without defenses to facilitate the sacrifice, lived under this sign: TO SERVE. She served in an exemplary way, to the prisoners, to the children who in the war needed a little food and much love; to the survivors of Málaga—who on the road to Almería were followed by cannon fire from German ships and bombs from Italian planes. Those who in Madrid in November of 1936 were together will never forget how Tina, surrounded by rubbish, bodies and dismembered limbs, how busy, diligent and serene she was in attending those most badly wounded.[4]

It was in Madrid that she received the news of the death of her mother, and we can imagine her anguish at being so far away from her family, to which she was devoted. In the spring of 1937 Tina was in Valencia for a Congress for the Defense of Culture Against Fascism. Among those attending were people like André Malraux from France and Pablo Neruda from Chile. Also present was a group of Mexicans, the poets Juan de la Cabada and the very young Octavio Paz; Silvestre Revueltas, musician; Angélica Arenal de Siqueiros, the wife of David Alfaro Siqueiros who was also in Spain, came to attend the conference and met Tina there. She had not known her during the previous years in Mexico. "For me," Angélica recalls, "there was a romantic aura about Tina. I had heard much of her history from David himself. She was the first person I met in Valencia. I found her very thin, still very beautiful, and very feminine. We did not talk of Mexico, nor of Tina's photography, because we were both immersed in what we each felt was an historic moment." Juan de la Cabada also remembers meeting her at that time—he had known her in Mexico in the twenties—and recalls that she seemed very pale, "talking but a little in a low-pitched voice; that lovely Spanish with the Italian lilt which added to its charm."

"How well I remember Tina in Mexico," Fernando Gamboa reminisced recently.

> In fact I remember her perfectly, when I first met her in 1929, with her hair tied at the back, her bright large sad eyes—her eyes were always shining but at the same time there was a melancholy look in them. She wore low-heeled shoes, a simple blouse and a black or blue skirt. She was loving and cordial, with a sweet, low voice and very affectionate. Everyone whom she considered her friend or comrade was treated with lots of care and love. When I first met her—I of course knew who she was—I was very young, but she was a woman who had already struggled a lot and participated in many things. She was a foreigner and she was surrounded by a kind of halo. The photograph which Weston made of her—it is like a symbol of Tina's personality and I am deeply touched by it [p. 64]. Tina sitting in a doorway. . . . I think she was always a woman with a tragic sense of life, even though she knew how to laugh and to be happy. She had been oppressed, she had suffered humiliation. Her enemies said awful things about her. She was very beautifully Italian, lovely skin, jet black hair, a woman besieged by men. Many women know

how to handle men who surround them. The miserable enemies are those men who do not obtain what they want and because of this rejection they put the woman down and say ugly things about her. . . . She was a woman who had come from the United States where we know she lived a life like many other young girls who had been in glamorous Hollywood during that period.* I think it was an infamy and a calumny to say that Tina was an easy woman. She was like so many others, some of them Mexican women who followed her example. There was a kind of beauty and personality that was fashionable during that period—if we are right in remembering that the Soviets created a style that they called the proletarian beauty, all simplicity, without any make-up.

I didn't see her again until I met her during the Spanish Civil War. That was in 1937. A group of Mexicans were invited to the Congress for the Defense of Culture Against Fascism held in Valencia. I met Tina at the offices of the newspaper *Ayuda.* I had been familiar with her life up until the time of her expulsion from Mexico and I never imagined we were going to meet again so unexpectedly. I recognized her sooner than she did me; it was, after all, a long time since we had last met. I asked after her health and of course inquired about her work—she explained that she was working more as a correspondent than as a photographer and was very much on the move.

His impressions of Tina at these two different times of her life were very strong in his memory.

---

*Of course the "actress" syndrome of the 1920's was even more effective in Mexico than in the United States during the "Jazz Age," with its implications of immortality and sexual freedom.

By the spring of 1938, it appeared to the outside world that the war in Spain was over. The leaders of Republican Spain were in exile, and France and England had given official recognition to the Nationalists. However, Herbert Matthews states categorically that "the Spanish Civil War ended on April 1, 1939."[5]

The Red Aid newspaper *Ayuda* was still being published in Madrid in August, 1938; there were many still fighting the cause of the Loyalists. Catalonia had been cut off from Madrid for many months and communication was almost impossible. Yet on November 1st, a National Congress of Solidarity took place in Madrid. Twelve-hundred delegates—among whom were Socialists, Communists, Anarchists, Republicans, those without parties, men and women, civilians and soldiers—had come together. This was a union of the front with the rear guard, of the battlefield with the factory and the land, of the people with their government. The Congress was opened before an international delegation. Meanwhile, aid came in the form of food and clothing through the few free roads open to Madrid. The enemy shelled the city that night. It was one of the most tragic of the war; Tina went from hospital to hospital looking for her friends and helping them receive proper care. Among the wounded, with grave injuries, was her own companion, Carlos Contreras.[6]

Tina had never remained in one place; she had been in Pozoblanco when the whole of Andalusia was under the threat of the invader; in Valencia when the fate of that city was uncertain; in Caspe at the time of the disaster of the Aragon front (1937); in Lérida and in Barbastro when the enemy was besieging Barcelona (March 1938); in Extremadura when the enemy broke through the Republican lines; in the retreat from Catalonia when the army withdrew to the border covering the tragic exodus of the population. In fact, Fernando Gamboa recalls:

I didn't see her again until the army retreat . . . I was one of the last Mexicans to leave Spain with the great Catalonian retreat; we left with Col. Adalberto Tejada, the Mexican Ambassador at that time—he behaved so bravely in Spain. I had been informed that a very important hidden archive of tapes and films had been left at the Castillo de Figueras. My wife (at that time) and I were given use of the Mexican Embassy car. Everything had been bombed the day before because the last Cortes of the Second Spanish Republic had been held in Figueras and the people who were leaving Barcelona were pouring into the city even though the *franquistas* bombed the city as well as the people who were on their way to France. It must have been in February. I went to the Castle, an enormous Gothic building, probably of the thirteenth or fourteenth century, and we found tapes and film, but actually this was unused material and not what we were looking for. I headed for another town nearby—about twenty minutes by car—but the town was nearly empty and I could not find what I was looking for. So I went to the center, and there, to my surprise, sitting alone at one of those outdoor coffee shops, was Tina. I asked, "What are you doing here?" "Just waiting," she replied. We embraced affectionately. She was waiting for the army which was on its way to that small town and she knew that Carlos was coming with it. I told her that she was in great danger and that she could not go along with the army—I even added as a joke, you are not in Mexico, you can't be a *soldadera* (camp follower). I tried to persuade her to come with me—the car we had at our disposal was large and carried the Mexican flag—in a half hour we could be in Guyana, which was where the embassy was set up; many people had gone through there already. I see her now—a different Tina—a tired woman; she was feeling the agony of the defeat, she realized what the disaster of the Republic meant, the Republic for which she had worked and fought. Even I, younger than Tina, strong and not tired, was in a very different situation. I was a Mexican who was trying to help, but she was in the same situation as the Spaniards and foreigners who were there to fight and were now dispossessed—without a country, defeated, and obliged to run away. Well, she refused my offer firmly; I wished her luck; I sent my greetings to Carlos and hoped that I would see them both again. I left, it was more or less at about six in the evening, the sun was shining but gave no warmth. The whole scene, the entire situation reinforced by the winter sun, the peasants escaping from the mountains, the army retreating and the image of Tina, sitting alone, with that waiting, searching, contemplative look—it seems to me that it is like the photograph which Weston made of Tina in Mexico—sitting alone and waiting . . .

And so Tina became one of thousands of refugees who, with a perfectly valid false passport declaring her to be Carmen

Ruiz Sánchez, left Figueras, Spain, with a visa from the Agence Consular de France. After seven weeks of living in camps, she went to Paris and there received a visa to leave for Mexico, which had aligned itself with the Republican cause and which opened its frontiers to refugees from Spain regardless of their nationality. She had also been given a transit visa allowing her to stay in the United States from the time of her arrival on April 16th until the end of June. When the "Queen Mary" arrived in New York, both Carlos Contreras and her sister Yolanda were there to meet her. But transit visa not withstanding, Tina was not allowed to disembark. She arrived in Vera Cruz, Mexico, on April 19, 1939—almost a decade after she had been expelled.

The bier with Weston's photograph of Tina.

1939-1942
Refuge in Mexico

5 The Mexico to which she returned was both familiar and yet strange. The pain of exile was to be borne not only by those who were political refugees from Spain and Italy but also by those from all the European countries who were the victims of Nazism. Mexico was at once a haven for the broadest spectrum of nationality and political definition: leftists of all persuasions, as well as active Nazis, Fascists and Franco supporters.

The political ferment of the entire world in this pre-World War II period was to be felt in Mexico. It seemed as though the suspicions, quarrels, retributions from abroad were being re-enacted in Mexico. It is normal for exiles to unite, particularly with language as a bond. But the quarrels and recriminations among the refugees from the Spanish Civil War became almost unbearable and the situation had become so muddled that one could hardly distinguish friend from foe.

Once in Mexico and reunited with Carlos Contreras, who had arrived there before Tina (he kept his *nom de guerre* all through his stay in Mexico), she earned a living by translating, while Carlos worked for the Communist newspaper *El Popular*. She lived quietly, and continued her political activities through the Anti-Fascist Alliance Giuseppe Garibaldi. She remained convinced that while she loved Mexico, Italy was her country. She always planned to return there after the defeat of Fascism, which she felt sure would come in her lifetime. They had close and trusted friends in Mexico, among whom were Verna Carlton and Ignacio Millán, Hannes Meyer, the architect who had been in Germany as director of the Bauhaus, Simone Téry, Pablo and Dalia Neruda. With these friends they would spend quiet evenings discussing the political situation abroad or listening to music.

It was not in the character of this honest woman to live under an assumed name in a country she loved. Maria, as she had been called in Spain by all who knew her, was her *nom de guerre*, and she was proud of it. But Carmen Ruiz Sanchez had no reality at all. Through the intervention of the same Adalberto Tejada who had helped her in Spain, she was able to regain the use of her own name, and it was through Tejada's interest and intervention that the government of Lázaro Cárdenas annulled the expulsion of 1930. Tina proudly resumed her name and with it, interestingly, she returned to the camera. Mexico itself had changed, but the country outside of Mexico City must have struck a responsive chord and she was eager to accept an assignment. In Cárdenas' Mexico of the early 1940's, Tina's political life had probably reached another turning point. Perhaps she did not now feel the need to subordinate her work in photography to political action. In any case, her political activity must have diminished in Mexico, where the battle for the revolution seemed to have been submerged in the larger battles raging throughout the world. Therefore, her return to the camera at this time is understandable.

For a book which was to have been written by Constancia de la Mora, another Spanish refugee, she went off again to record with her own vision and sensitivity the arts and crafts of Mexico and the people who produced them in their own environment. Alas, the book never appeared and the negatives have vanished.

Among the friends who had known her in the past and who saw her on occasion at this time, Fernando Gamboa states,

Tina is a wonderful example of the personality of a woman during that most difficult period in world history. There is no doubt that she was a great artist— her photographs reveal this—with an extraordinary sensibility, an exquisite, clear vision. If she was not an intellectual in the literary sense of the word, she was a woman forged by universal discipline; she was obviously an intellectual, as any real artist has to be. Even though Weston had great influence in shaping Tina's artistic vision, her photographs are in no sense similar to Weston's. He had a very different sense of space, he had an extraordinary technique, a whole sense of composition. Tina's photographs show a kind of human obsession, and her tragic sense of life can be seen in her work.

When I last saw Tina—here in Mexico right after the

Tina's funeral

day on which the United States declared war—she was so tired, she seemed so ill, her skin seemed grey and spotted.

It is hardly surprising that Tina—her energies and emotions diminished by the hardships of the last years—appeared tired. Hannes Meyer best describes Tina's last evening:

> "*Arrivederci,*" she said to me with a handshake. That was on January 5th (1942) at midnight, as she left my house. We all—three married couples—had been talking for hours about everything we admired: the genius of Simeon Timoshenko, the Soviet anti-tank trenches, Shostakovich's Quintet Op. 57 . . . and discussing the possibility of a trip from Madrid, Geneva and Udine to Moscow . . . without passports. "*Arrivederci,*" she said again with a smile, and disappeared quickly into the dark night.
>
> Ten minutes later she was in a taxicab, motionless, cold, alone. Alive when she took the cab, dead when she was taken out of it. . . .

Carlos had left the dinner party somewhat earlier in the evening to go to the office of *El Popular* before he planned to join Tina at home. She took a taxi and was alone when the tragedy occurred—a massive heart attack took her life. The driver was terrified, and abandoned the taxi; the police then brought her to the *Cruz Verde* (Green Cross), where friends came later to identify the body.

In death as in life Tina became headline news, and the calumny continued. She became the victim of unjust accusations; gossip mongers speculated freely. It was rumored that she had been poisoned, and some even claimed that the poison had been administered by her own friends. It was whispered that she knew too much about the still unresolved assassination of Mella. It seemed impossible that she would not be touched by the jungle of suspicion and rage that was Mexico in that fateful year, 1942. The stories of her expulsion were revived, and the rumors went on unabated, but, as Margarita Nelken had said, "Nothing elevates so much as the attack of the enemy—there is no crown more resplendent than that of thorns."

Unknown to most people but known to Carlos was the fact that Tina had had a slight history of heart difficulties while in Europe. Alvarez Bravo discounts the rumors of poisoning. He quite easily accepts the fact that after a heavy meal Tina suffered coronary failure due to indigestion and, given the lack of medical knowledge in that time with regard to heart treatment, she died before medication could be given.

Nothing, it seems, stood between Tina and the pursuit of the astonishing goals she set for herself—only her own death, which was mourned wherever her life and struggles were known. The funeral was attended by thousands: close friends and comrades, workers, representatives of trade unions, women's groups, and government officials, who followed her flower-covered casket (with the photograph of Tina by Weston) to the Pantheon of Dolores in Mexico, where she is buried.

On February 23 of 1942, a posthumous homage took place in the *Teatro del Pueblo*, followed by an exhibition of her photographs at the *Inez Amor Galería de Arte*. On this occasion Manuel Alvarez Bravo, her long-time friend and fellow photographer, wrote:

More than by death, Tina's work was cut short by the fact that her life had gone in other directions; still, in the short time that she was an active photographer, she was able to create a body of work which remains the lesson of her understanding and her love of the methods and orientation most appropriate to the field . . . She combined human document, technical maturity, plastic surety, mastery of her medium; all these brought together in this exhibition, which is both a stimulus and an homage.

At the same time, a brochure was published in which many wrote their tributes to her. For this occasion, and dedicated to Carlos Contreras, the Chilean Pablo Neruda wrote his poem "Tina Modotti has died," which contains the essence of Tina:

Perfect your gentle name, perfect your fragile life—
bees, shadows, fire, snow, silence and foam combining
with steel and wire and pollen to make up your firm
and delicate being.

TINA MODOTTI
1896 – 1942

Tina Modotti, hermana,
no duermes, no, no duermes:
tal vez tu corazón
oye crecer la rosa
de ayer, la última rosa
de ayer, la nueva rosa.
Descansa dulcemente,
hermana.

Pura es tu dulce nombre,
pura es tu frágil vida:
de abeja, sombra, fuego,
nieve, silencio, espuma,
de acero, línea, polen,
se construyó tu férrea,
tu delgada estructura...

PABLO NERUDA

Tina's tombstone in the Pantheon of Dolores, Mexico, D.F.

LIST OF ILLUSTRATIONS

BIBLIOGRAPHY

Note: the following is not an exhaustive bibliography but a list of publications which the author has directly quoted or consulted.

Brenner, Anita. *Idols Behind Altars*, Boston, 1970.
——. *The Wind that Swept Mexico*, New York and London, 1943.
Creative Arts. Issue of February, 1929.
Dubos, Rene. *A God Within*, New York, 1972.
Dulles, John W. F. *Yesterday in Mexico*, Austin, 1961.
International Literature (Moscow). Vol. 12, 1935; Vol. 1, 1936.
Maddow, Ben. *Edward Weston: Fifty Years*, New York, 1974.
Matthews, Herbert. *The Yoke and the Arrow: A Report on Spain*, London, 1958.
Mexican Folkways (Mexico, D.F.). Edited by Frances Toor.
Myers, Bernard. *Modern Art in the Making*, New York, 1950.
Newhall, Nancy, Ed. *The Daybooks of Edward Weston: Vol. I (Mexico), Vol. II (California)*, New York, 1961.
Niemeyer, E. V. *Revolution at Querétaro*, Austin, 1974.
Orozco, Jose Clemente. *The Artist in New York: Letters to Jean Charlot and other unpublished writings* (1925–1929), Austin and London, 1974.
Radin, Paul. *The Italians of San Francisco: Their Adjustment and Acculturation*, Works Progress Administration, 1935.
Rollo, Andrew. *The Immigrant Upraised: Italian Adventures and Colonists in an Expanding America*, New York, 1968.
Rexroth, Kenneth. *An Autobiographical Novel*, Garden City, 1966.
Richey, Tina Modotti. *The Book of Robo*, with an Introduction by John Cowper Powys, Los Angeles, 1923.
Rivera, Diego. *My Art, My Life: An Autobiography*, New York, 1960.
——. *The Frescoes of Diego Rivera* (Introduction by Ernestine Evans), New York, 1929.
Shirer, William. *The Rise and Fall of the Third Reich*, New York, 1960.
Thomas, Hugh. *The Spanish Civil War*, New York, 1961.
Vidali, Vittorio. *Il Quinto Reggimento*, Milan, 1973.
Von Passen, Pierre. *Days of our Years*, New York, 1939.
Wolfe, Bertram. *The Fabulous Life of Diego Rivera*, New York, 1963.

The Circolo Culturale "Elio Mauro" has published *Tina Modotti, Garibaldina e artista* (Udine, Italy, 1973).

FOOTNOTES

CHAPTER I
[1] Kenneth Rexroth, *An Autobiographical Novel* (Garden City, 1966), p. 344.
[2] Rene Dubos, *A God Within* (New York, 1972), pp. 122–123.
[3] Tina Modotti Richéy, *The Book of Robo* with an introduction by John Cowper Powys (Los Angeles, 1923).
[4] *The Daybooks of Edward Weston*, Edited by Nancy Newhall (New York, 1961).
[5] Richéy, *loc. cit.*
[6] *Daybooks*, Introduction.
[7] Ben Maddow, *Edward Weston: Fifty Years* (New York, 1974).
[8] Anita Brenner, *The Wind that Swept Mexico* (New York and London, 1943), p. 57.
[9] Bernard Myers, *Modern Art in the Making* (New York, 1950).

CHAPTER II
[1] *Daybooks*, p. 13.
[2] Diego Rivera, *My Art, My Life: An Autobiography* (New York, 1960), pp. 161–162.
[3] *Daybooks*, p. 95.
[4] *ibid*, p. 101.
[5] *Mexican Folkways* (April–May, 1926).

CHAPTER III
[1] Maddow, *op. cit.*, p. 49.
[2] *Daybooks*, p. 119.
[3] Jose Clemente Orozco, *The Artist in New York: Letters to Jean Charlot and other unpublished writings* (1925–1929) (Austin and London, 1974).

CHAPTER IV
[1] John W. F. Dulles, *Yesterday in Mexico* (Austin, 1961), pp. 484–485.
[2] William Shirer, *The Rise and Fall of the Third Reich* (New York, 1960), p. 122.
[3] Vittorio Vidali, *Il Quinto Reggimento* (Milan, 1973).
[4] Hugh Thomas, *The Spanish Civil War* (New York, 1961).
[5] *Tina Modotti, Garibaldina e artista* (Udine, 1973).
[6] Herbert Matthews, *The Yoke and the Arrows: A Report on Spain* (London, 1958).
[7] Vidali, *loc cit.*

INDEX

223